AFTER SUICIDE

CHRISTIAN CARE BOOKS

Wayne E. Oates, Editor

AFTER SUICIDE

by

John H. Hewett

THE WESTMINSTER PRESS
Philadelphia

Book Design by Dorothy Alden Smith

Published by The Westminster Press®
Philadelphia, Pennsylvania

PRINTED IN THE UNITED STATES OF AMERICA
10   11   12   13   14   15

Library of Congress Cataloging in Publication Data

Hewett, John H 1952–
    After suicide.

    (Christian care books ; no. 4)
    Bibliography: p.
    1. Suicide. 2. Suicide—Psychological aspects.
3. Suicide—Moral and religious aspects. 4. Bereavement. 5. Consolation. I.Title. II. Series.
HV6545.H45   155.9'37   79–24373
ISBN 0–664–24296–0

Contents

Preface

A member of your immediate family or the larger family of those dear to you has purposely ended his or her life. Your loved one has been permanently torn away, leaving a gaping wound in your life that you may doubt will ever heal. Now you are left behind to undergo the agony of acute bereavement, a grief punctuated by spasms of guilt, anger, bewilderment, and shame. Suicide, that whispered taboo which only happens to other families, has happened to yours.

This little book has been written to help you in the aftermath. It's too late to stop the suicide that has scarred your life. The time for *"pre*vention" or *"inter*vention" has passed. However, the time is right to begin your crucial process of *"post*vention"—that process after a suicide during which your family works toward emotional recovery and readjustment to healthy living. The suicidal death of your family member forces you to ask different questions, express unusual emotions, and face difficult fears. That's why "postvention" is for you.

Edwin Shneidman, foremost American expert on suicide and developer of the term "postvention," describes the burden that a suicide places upon the surviving family.

11

I believe that the person who commits suicide puts his psychological skeleton in the survivor's emotional closet—he sentences the survivor to deal with many negative feelings, and, more, to become obsessed with thoughts regarding his own actual or possible role in having precipitated the suicidal act or having failed to abort it. It can be a heavy load. (Edwin S. Shneidman, "Foreword," in Albert C. Cain, ed., *Survivors of Suicide*, p. x; Charles C Thomas, 1972)

Indeed, it is often an almost unbearable load. That's why this book came into being. I want to help you along the way toward surviving this tragedy, and through you to assist your family as well.

A few words need to be said about the language of this book. I have avoided using the word "commit" with regard to suicide. This word gives a connotation of criminality that I believe is unnecessary and undesirable. Current literature on the subject divides suicidal actions into "attempted" and "completed" suicides, and I have continued this usage.

I am assuming that the most frequent readers of this book will be women whose husbands or sons have completed suicide. Three times as many men complete suicide as women, and so a large proportion of the readers of this book are probably wives or mothers.

I am writing as a Christian minister and a Christian ethicist, and this perspective is evident throughout the book. My prayer, however, is that this viewpoint might be secondary to the help included here for *all* suicide survivors, regardless of religious persuasion.

Some words of appreciation are in order. My wife, June Martin Hewett, has been supportive of this effort throughout the process, and has made valuable suggestions from a woman's point of view. The Elmburg Baptist Church in Elmburg, Kentucky, undergirded me in many ways during the writing of this book, not the least of which was the willingness of those dear people to guard my time for education and writing. The several families of suicides who consented to meet with me and preview the manuscript have invested their grief that you might regain the joy of healthy living.

Finally, I must thank my esteemed teacher, Wayne Oates. He called forth this work from me in his own serendipitous fashion and pledged both his time and his heart in the writing. But, more importantly, he has incarnated for me the healing love of Jesus Christ. He has invited me into both his past and his future, as a comrade and fellow sojourner. Wayne Oates has "shown me the Father."

J.H.H.

Graefenburg Baptist Church
Waddy,Kentucky

1. Getting the Facts Straight

The silently awkward aftermath of suicide is often churned up by a vague, shadowy, threatening fear of the unknown. Questions plague you and your family: Why did she do it? What could have made him so depressed? What will happen to the children? Why didn't I prevent it? What was he thinking about? Didn't she love us enough to spare us this agony? What on earth does this suicide note mean?

Fear can grip you with strong, unyielding clutches. It threatens to heighten your anxiety and emotionally disable you. You can begin to face it. You must meet "the enemy" face to face. You can confront this gnawing sense of panic by getting the facts straight about suicide—finding out the whats, hows, whys, and wherefores. You will put some of these questions to rest. Thus you will protect yourself against the avalanche of half-truths, cultural myths, and superstitions that rain down in the aftermath.

Like any profoundly mysterious event, suicide has acquired a mythology all its own. This chapter will help you debunk some of those myths. You can bring the subject of suicide into the clear light of day and begin to *learn* about the tragedy that has overtaken your family. Once you begin to learn, you can

15

begin to heal. Know the truth about suicide—it is essential
to your recovery. That means getting the facts straight.

A Long Look Backward

You are going to feel a constant temptation to take a short
backward look. Take a long one instead. People have been
purposely taking their lives for thousands of years. Suicide
shows up in all kinds of societies and throughout every histori-
cal epoch. It is as ancient as humanity itself. It occurred
among the ancient Hebrews. The Greeks and Romans also
were plagued with the problem of self-destruction. They held
a hard-line position opposing it, except for the Stoics and
Epicureans, who adopted a softer approach. The early Christian church was forced to take stern measures to deal with the
epidemic of suicides that took place. So many believers were
eager to gain heavenly glory that martyrdoms became commonplace. Augustine, and later Thomas Aquinas, labeled suicide a mortal sin equivalent to murder. With a few exceptions, they gave the church's sanction to the civil laws against
the act.

The attitude of condemnation did not ease until the period
of the Enlightenment in the eighteenth century. Then
philosophers like Hume and Voltaire began to stress the pri-
macy of individual freedom and the consequent "right" to
suicide. A huge mass of legal punishments that had accumulated over the centuries stood in their way. Legal taboos
compounded the private grief of suicide survivors. They were
afflicted by brutal cultural rituals and religious stigma. For
centuries, the act of suicide was met by stiff and rigid punishment. All property belonging to the victim was forfeited to

the state. The surviving family was left homeless and desti-
tute. Burial in consecrated ground was refused by the church.
The body was frequently maimed and desecrated in acts of
unspeakable violence. Families were socially "branded." They
were often forced to move from their communities in order
to retain their own sanity.

Gradually the laws began to ease, under the influence of
both the learned people and the church. You can begin to be
thankful that, in some ways, we humans are at last becoming
more humane. Currently, none of the few remaining laws
against attempted suicide are being enforced. No legal punishment exists for the families of suicide victims. The empha-
sis in this country has shifted from viewing suicide as a crime
to seeing it as a *sickness.* Thus we see a widespread intensifi-
cation of effort for suicide prevention. The potential suicide
is seen as an object of concern and medical intervention
rather than as a potential felon.

Unfortunately, this more compassionate approach to the
problem has largely overlooked the families of suicidal individuals. There are few hot lines to call after the suicide has
happened! The coroner's inquest and the autopsy are usually
thought to be the only necessary follow-up procedures. Your
family is quickly forgotten. That's why this book has been
written. I want to help you take your place in the company
of people who have been hit with the blow of suicide and still
survived. You are not alone. A great deal can be done to help
you in your own process of getting yourself back together
again. Millions have come through this crisis, and you can as
well. My hope is that this volume can minister to you in both
fact and feeling. We will look at feelings in the remainder of
the book. But first we will check out the data on the subject.

Suicide Statistics

Actor Jack Webb will forever be remembered for his legendary *Dragnet* character, Sgt. Joe Friday. This deadpan, "strictly business" detective always wanted "just the facts, Ma'am." For the families of suicide victims, the Joe Friday approach to the tragedy can be an initial move toward emotional recovery. The bereavement of survivors like yourself often becomes dangerously harmful if the persistent fears of the unknown "enemy" aren't dispelled by the assurance of accurate information. Such fears are often fueled by varieties of shared misinformation and all-too-common knowledge, as well as the severe emotional aftershock of the suicide itself. A first step toward recovery is unlearning what is not so.

You have a right to know the truth about the suicide that happened to your family. You can place that knowledge in healthy perspective by learning the available details about suicide in general. Dependable information needs to be secured from competent professionals, not from uninformed friends or backyard philosophers. What follows are "just the facts." I hope they will speak knowledge and the assurance of truth into the silently fearful aftermath of suicide.

No one knows precisely how many persons choose to end their lives each year. Official suicide statistics are notoriously unreliable. They are unreliable because thousands of suicides go unreported every year. If you question why accurate data cannot be accumulated on the prevalence of suicide in this country, several reasons can be readily identified. First, families often go to great lengths to suppress the fact of suicide. They fear the resulting social stigma. Perhaps they are concerned to preserve life insurance claims that might otherwise be declared invalid. Many factors prompt secrecy among surviving families. Second, methods of reporting suicides are inconsistent from region to region. One California coroner would declare a death to be self-inflicted only if a suicide note was found! Third, 15 to 20 percent of investigated deaths are ambiguous, with causes usually ruled either accident or suicide. These deaths are quite difficult to identify. They include such equivocal causes as single-car crashes, drownings, and wounds sustained during hunting and gun-cleaning "accidents." Fourth, our country contains a huge class of persons who knowingly hasten or cause their own deaths through chronic alcohol or drug abuse, unnecessary risk-taking, and even the initiation of their own murders. Death certificates would not list any of these as suicidal deaths, but often they are clear cases of willful self-destruction.

The latest reports of the United States Public Health Service on "officially" designated suicides indicate that 28,000–30,000 Americans purposely take their lives each year. Experts claim that the actual total is closer to three times that, with suicide *attempts* approaching eight to ten times the completed rate. Possibly as many as one million people attempt suicide in this country each year. These statistics indicate that millions of Americans alive today have on at least one occasion attempted to take their own lives. As many as 90,000–100,000 persons probably complete suicide each year in this country. If we assume a realistic average of five family members for each suicidal death, then our nation includes 150,000–500,000 suicide survivors involved in "postvention" at any one time. And those are only members of the immediate family! Clearly, you are not alone in your unique grief situation.

Suicide is a public health crisis. It ranks among the top ten causes of death among American adults. It is currently the second highest cause of death among adolescents and children, surpassed only by accidents. These self-inflicted deaths cost our cities and states billions of dollars annually in emergency facilities, hospitalization, and loss of income. More Americans die at their own hands than are killed in acts of homicide. For those over sixty-five, suicide is a major killer. Though these older adults comprise only 10 percent of the total population, they account for 25 percent of all the reported suicides each year. Failing health, the shrinking value of a fixed income, and stifling loneliness often combine to make suicide an alluring alternative to our nation's elderly.

Although women *attempt* suicide three times as frequently as men, men *complete* suicide three times as often as women. Though some recent evidence points to a change in this ratio toward a more equal proportion between the sexes, the fact remains that men do follow through on their destructive intentions more seriously than do women.

White-collar professionals in leadership positions are greater risks than blue-collar laborers and farmers. Among professionals, medical doctors (especially psychiatrists) are thought to kill themselves at a much higher rate than others, with female physicians more vulnerable than their male colleagues. Such data remains in question at present, with research studies supporting both sides of the debate.

Divorced persons take their lives more often than singles; single individuals complete suicide more often than married persons.

The suicide rate of white Americans has historically outnumbered that of blacks, but the black rate is rising. American Indians have an unusually high suicide rate. This may date from the inclusion of suicide in primitive tribal rituals, as with the Navajo, who prescribed suicide as punishment for breaking a taboo.

Suicide rates increase geographically as you move from east to west, with much higher totals in cities than in rural areas. The mountain and Pacific states report the highest national incidence of suicide. The "fever spots" in the West are Las Vegas, Los Angeles, and San Francisco. It should not be surprising that the suicidal People's Temple cult was centered in San Francisco; that city is the "suicide capital" of the nation, with a rate two and a half times the national average. Other high-risk areas in this country include Miami and St. Petersburg, the Florida geriatric centers, where rates approach twice the national average.

April and May are the peak months for suicides. Evidently this reflects the suicidal person's despair and anxiety, which seem so totally at odds with the rebirth of spring and the reminder of things fresh and new. Except for a brief upsurge during the stressful Christmas season, the rate decreases in winter, when the weather more accurately reflects the victim's mood.

A suicide is more likely to occur at home during the early morning and early evening hours. It happens most often on Friday and Monday, when the pressures of another lonely weekend or a dreaded workweek loom largest.

Guns and explosives are the most common methods used in self-inflicted death. Lethal overdoses of medication are the second choice. Men tend toward the more violent means of suicide, while women usually choose the less often lethal path of the drug overdose. The grim list of other suicidal methods defies the imagination. Such methods break the boundaries of the bizarre, as human beings take their lives by a limitless variety of means.

Suicide rates plummet during wartime, but rise sharply during periods of severe economic crisis and high unemployment. This was shown in America during the Great Depression of the 1930's.

Currently, in its rate of reported suicides, the United States ranks in about the middle of the list of countries reporting to the United Nations. Austria, West Germany, Hungary, Japan, Czechoslovakia, Denmark, Finland, Sweden, and Switzerland report significantly higher rates than ours. Italy, the Netherlands, and Spain indicate far fewer suicides than are reported by the United States.

Unlearning What Is Not So About Suicide

A learned professor of mine once remarked that he knew of nothing more frightening than ignorance in action. Such a judgment certainly applies to the abundance of superstitious fallacies and cultural fantasies that have grown up around the problem of suicide.

You may have already discovered that some people are quick to offer advice to those whom they perceive as helpless. They will readily dispense timeworn clichés about your situation with little tact and even less forethought. They give you a mishmash of fables and fantasies that have been proved wrong. In unlearning things that are not so, you defuse the potentially explosive effects of these myths. Fantasies *and* facts are offered here with the hope that this information will assist you and your family in separating truth from fiction.

Myth: "People who talk about killing themselves never do."

Fact: Fully 80 percent of all completed suicides do in fact speak of their intentions beforehand. Sometimes they threaten or hint of suicide until those around them grow weary of the persistent "promises." Or, they confide in one or two close friends, or perhaps their physicians or ministers. Suicide hot lines all across the country report thousands upon thousands of calls each year, which certainly indicate that suicidal persons do indeed want to talk about their despair and feelings of panic. As you reflect upon the last months and weeks before the suicide in your family, you may begin to recall the scattered hints and vague allusions given out by the victim. Certainly you remember the obvious threats and cries for help if they were given.

Myth: "Suicide usually happens without warning, 'on the spur of the moment.'"

Fact: This misconception is closely tied with the first, in the attempt to portray suicide as but another type of sudden death. It is commonly bandied about in informal discussions, and often used to give consolation to the grieving family—the "you had no way of knowing" approach. You do not derive solace from this kind of misinformation unless it actually *was* impossible for you to know about the impending suicide. For example, you may have been hundreds of miles away at the time. Research shows that suicidal individuals offer many clues and warnings, not all of which are verbal, regarding the growing intention to self-destruct. Very few suicides ever happen "out of the blue." What appears to be the result of a sudden, momentary impulse usually is the culmination of a long history of crises and traumas within the victim's life. Clues are often given to family and friends by an increase in accidents and unnecessary risk-taking, or by a marked change in eating, sleeping, or sexual activity.

Perhaps your family member truly did complete suicide totally without warning. You truthfully had no way of knowing. This does happen when family members are separated by time and distance, but such instances do not validate this second myth. If your family member did decide to die "on the spur of the moment," try to accept that as a rare occurrence. Resist the compulsion toward self-torment and blame. Incredible suicides such as these render all statistics irrelevant.

Myth: "All persons who attempt suicide are fully intent on dying."

Fact: Suicide attempts and suicidal "gestures" outnumber completed suicides by as much as ten to one. This illustrates the suicidal person's mixed motives and emotions. Many suicidal persons are undecided about whether to choose life or death. In one way or another they cry for help, and they hope someone rescues them before death occurs. Studies of suicide notes show that the feelings of unbearable tension and overwhelming ambivalence are common for many suicidal individuals. Certainly many a suicide results from an ill-calculated gamble with death, where the cry for help goes unheard or unheeded.

Myth: "If a person is suicidal once, he or she will continue to struggle with suicidal impulses forever."

Fact: Thousands of formerly suicidal individuals happily proclaim this cliché to be a fantasy. They claim that the period of highest risk is brief in duration. The greatest struggle comes during the immediate crisis and the period of readjustment that comes later. As Shneidman points out:

> The acute suicidal crisis, or period of high and dangerous lethality, is an interval of relatively short duration—to be counted, typically, in hours or days, not usually in terms of months or years. A person is at a peak of self-destructiveness for a brief time and then is helped, cools off, or is dead. Although one can live for years at a chronically elevated self-destructive level, one cannot have a loaded gun to one's head before either the bullet or the emotion is discharged. (Edwin S. Shneidman, "Suicide," in Alfred M. Freedman et al., eds., *Comprehensive Textbook of Psychiatry—II,* 2d ed., p. 1779; Williams & Wilkins Co., 1975)

This is, of course, scant comfort for the family of a completed suicide. It stresses once more the painful presence of willful choice and responsibility in the victim's decision to die. However, if one of your family members is currently having suicidal impulses as a result of this suicide, you need to assure him or her that help is available to endure the crisis period. Suicidal impulses are not a lifelong curse. You don't have to be haunted forever by the fatal urges you may be feeling at the moment. *You won't always feel this way.*

Myth: "Only a psychotic, 'crazy' person can actually go through with suicide."

Fact: The foremost experts on suicide are vehement in their denial of this fable. Although your family member may have felt extremely unhappy and anxious, to be sure, the act of suicide wasn't necessarily irrational or the product of an unbalanced mind. Many suicides are completed by persons whose minds are at the height of their capability but which are imprisoned within helpless, failing bodies. Now, we know that many psychotic persons do take their own lives. But this doesn't mean that all suicides are mentally ill. There is little consolation in the knowledge that one's family member completed suicide while insane. Rather, as Rabbi Earl Grollman points out, "telling the survivors that the person was crazy does not add to their social status . . . [nor] lighten the burden; it only brings the fear of inherited mental disease" (Earl Grollman, *Suicide: Prevention, Intervention, Postvention*, p. 114; Beacon Press, 1971).

Myth: "Suicide is inherited, or runs in the family."

Fact: This contention cannot be supported by the facts. Although there are many psychological and social reasons why one suicide in a family can lead to another, no evidence exists in support of a genetic predisposition toward suicide or any sort of biological programming toward self-destruction. As Edwin Shneidman vigorously asserts, "suicide is an individual pattern" (Shneidman, "Suicide," p. 1780).

Myth: "Suicide is the rich man's disease; or, suicide is the poor woman's 'way out.' "

Fact: Suicide occurs on all levels of society and can be encountered in every neighborhood. The emotional distress that leads to suicide is not unique to either Bedford-Stuyvesant or Westchester County, Watts or Beverly Hills. It can happen to anyone, anywhere.

Myth: "Every 'true' suicide leaves a suicide note."

Fact: Only about 15 percent of those who complete suicides leave notes, in stark contrast to the stereotypical suicides of television and motion pictures. This harmful misconception has led to widespread underreporting of suicidal deaths, under the assumption that the absence of a note means death either by accident, homicide, or natural causes.

Myth: "You should never talk about suicide to a depressed person; you could give him or her ideas."

Fact: If a person is truly severely depressed, the thought of suicide won't need to come from outside—it has probably already risen from within, either to be quickly banished or grimly pondered. You don't give a suicidal person lethal ideas by talking about the subject. Rather, you provide an opportunity for ventilation of those feelings by getting them out into the open. If I suspect that a person is thinking of suicide, I ask him about it right then. If he admits to having suicidal thoughts, I try to get him to agree to avoid such action. This may or may not prevent suicide, but it opens the issue and secures my concern. Remember, the "ideas" cannot be confronted once the suicide has already happened.

Myths and fables such as these cloud the issue of suicide

by allowing people to delude themselves, to push away the morbid feelings aroused by the subject, and to live as though their lives could never be scarred by suicide. But your life has been so scarred. Your first step toward recovery and psychological readjustment comes in dealing with the truth about this death, however painful and repulsive that truth might seem. Fear tends to dissipate when it is localized and confronted. Pain can be reduced by visualizing it and learning to control its ill effects. You can also learn to manage the shock of suicide by learning all you can about the "enemy." That's the first battle in quelling the war raging within you.

Explanations That Make Some Sense

Every suicide is different, and yet every suicide is the same. This is an enigmatic statement, to be sure. Yet it reflects the puzzle that suicide has historically presented the psychiatric community, the legal establishment, and the church. I could list a dozen established theories as to why people take their own lives, each supported by reputable men and women trained to observe such behavior. Some say that suicide is always an act of hostility turned inward. These views are in line with those of Sigmund Freud, who, as Edwin Shneidman points out, saw suicide as "murder in the 180th degree" (Shneidman, "Suicide," p. 1775).

Another group, identified with psychiatrist Karl Menninger, perceives suicide as driven by three types of hostility: the wish to kill, the wish to be killed, and the wish to die (Karl Menninger, *Man Against Himself;* Harcourt, Brace & World, 1966).

The classic sociological explanation was given by Emile

Durkheim in 1897, although this book was not translated into English until 1951 (Emile Durkheim, *Suicide: A Study in Sociology*, tr. by John Spaulding and George Simpson; Free Press, 1951). In his extended treatment, Durkheim identified three basic types of suicide, each caused by the person's relationship with society. The first type, *altruistic* suicide, Durkheim felt to be required by the social group under certain conditions. Included are the practices of hara-kiri (ritual suicide by disembowelment, formerly practiced by the Japanese upper classes) and suttee (the act, now forbidden by law, of a Hindu widow cremating herself on her husband's funeral pyre). The second type, *egoistic* suicide, describes most of the suicides in this country. These are completed by "loners" who have little investment in the life of their communities, churches, or families. The third type, *anomic* suicide, refers to suicides that come when a relationship between the victim and the society falls apart. Deaths of this kind occurred after the stock market crash in 1929, and are likely when a person cannot handle the loss of others close to him, according to this view.

This variety of theories underscores in what sense every suicide is different. But how is every suicide the same? As Shneidman shows clearly, a dozen persons can complete suicide for as many different reasons. "One was escaping from pain, another was afraid of going insane, a third acted on impulse after a quarrel, a fourth hoped to join a loved one in the hereafter, a fifth was punishing his parents, and so on." Yet a common, painful thread runs through each of these deaths: the "pressure of unbearable anguish" felt by the victim. In this sense, Shneidman says, "*every* case of overt self-destruction . . . is better understood as an *escape from* rather than a going toward" (Shneidman, "Suicide," p. 1774).

The best explanation of suicide about which I know deals with this question of escape. As Shneidman shows, the most common emotion in suicidal crisis is not hostility as much as it is *despair.* The suicidal person feels trapped in a corner by this overwhelming and unbearable mental pain. He or she eventually feels pushed to the point where "something must be done." Yet, even at that point, the person is gripped by mixed motives. "The psychodynamic heart of the suicidal act is *ambivalence;* the characteristic suicidal sound is the *cry for help;* the prototypical suicidal act is to cut one's throat and plead for help and fantasy rescue and intervention—all at the same time" (Shneidman, "Suicide," p. 1779).

More than likely, your family member was a confused and bewildered person suffering tremendous emotional pain. He or she probably wasn't choosing death as much as choosing to end this unbearable pain. The fact that no other option seemed to be possible testifies to the severe mental strain of your loved one. Like one trapped in a burning building, your family member probably saw suicide as a quick, effective way to stop the slow torture he or she was experiencing in life.

This common thread of intolerable despair isn't enough to make sense of all suicides. No explanation can hope to do that. What it does provide is a sketch of the illness at the core of our society that causes individuals to totally lose hope for a better life. You may not be able to understand this kind of thorough hopelessness. Not many do, unless they've been through it themselves. I hope you never have to have that experience.

This has been, in many ways, a frightening discussion. We have talked about the fact of widespread self-destruction in the midst of our nation and in the center of your family. I am reminded of Franklin Roosevelt's rallying cry to a fearful nation more than forty years ago. In the depths of an economic depression, our young and naive nation heard him proclaim that "the only thing we have to fear is fear itself." These are wise words for your family as well. The conquering of the fear that comes with suicide, the fear of the unknown, begins with getting the facts straight. Nothing may be more frightening than ignorance in action, as my teacher once told me, but there is nothing more encouraging than knowledge putting fear to flight.

2. Coping with Acute Grief: What to Expect

Grief is your response to a great loss in your life. When persons close to you die, you not only lose *them*—you also lose all the things they offered you in return. You lose the objects of your affection. Your love returns to you like a "dead letter" with no forwarding address. Grief is the feeling that comes in response to the experience of *amputation,* whether it be physical or emotional. It's your reaction to having part of your life cut off from you. Whether you lose an arm, or a close member of your family, the grief is similar: both are parts of *you,* and you mourn their loss with great sorrow and distress.

Most grief is anticipated. Family members know in advance that death is coming, and they begin their mourning before the actual moment of death. But *acute* grief, sudden grief, is like a fist slamming into your chest. It's unannounced, you're unprepared for the blow, and you're left battered and shaken in the aftermath.

Of course, not all suicide grief is *acute.* The degree of surprise involved varies from case to case. You may have already broken off your relationship with the deceased before the suicide, so your grief will be lessened. Or perhaps you had become "desensitized" to the death by repeated suicide attempts and cries of "Wolf!" But if you never expected either death or suicide, if you were a total stranger to this death, then your grief will be the most severe of all.

Acute, sudden grief hurts deeply. The pain will last a long time. You can't escape from it, but you can help it run its course. You must be willing to face the pain head-on, accepting the full force of it. Only by working through it, and sharing it with others, will you be able to finally let it go. That may be a couple of years down the road, if all goes well. During this time, you must be careful not to get "stuck" in your grieving by freezing the process at one particular spot.

Getting stuck in grief is like trying to drive in a winter ice storm. You know where you want to go, you know how to get there, but you find yourself miles away from your destination, helplessly spinning your wheels in one place. You find yourself frozen solid in an emotion from which you can't get free. If that happens, you'll need more help than this book can offer. A trained counselor will be able to help you work through this obstacle. Remember, you're the one who sets the pace and the limits of your grief. You can shorten or lengthen it, depending on your willingness to work through it.

In his important book on suicide bereavement, *Suicide and Grief* (Fortress Press, 1972), Howard Stone identifies seven phases of suicide grief which occur in most families. I want to modify his general framework slightly to help you see what you can expect in the weeks and months ahead. These different grief phases or stages do not occur automatically. Not every person will move directly from one to another. Your own phases of grief may not all occur in this order. However, almost everyone will experience these particular emotions sometime during suicide grief. The phases overlap, and will

even recur at later times. Take a good look at them now, and
begin to get ready to face them.

SHOCK

By the time you begin reading this book, you are probably
through with shock, the first stage of acute grief. During this
time you felt numb and cold, as if you were far away from
other people and out of touch with reality. Your mind was in
shock, just as your body would be if you suffered a serious
physical injury. In this stage, your mind anesthetized you
against the tremendous blow that hit you. You may have felt
as if you were in a dream, helpless to change the events
happening around you. You probably repeated over and over
again that you just couldn't believe it.

Physical symptoms are common in the stage of shock.
Survivors complain of tightness in the throat, upset stomach,
diarrhea, shortness of breath, and a general feeling of slowness
in moving around.

In these first few days of acute grief, you began to ask
yourself the questions that plague suicide survivors. Why did
this happen? What did I do to cause this? Was it my fault?
If you were a "stranger to death," you may have refused to
believe that the death was caused by suicide. Even in the face
of overwhelming evidence to the contrary, many survivors
deny the fact of suicide in the early days of shock. It's one
way of holding at arm's length the specter of pain and suffering coming your way.

Relief

Wayne Oates has pointed out in his treatment of acute grief, "Not all deaths are unwelcome" (Wayne E. Oates, *Pastoral Care and Counseling in Grief and Separation,* p. 52; Fortress Press, 1976). Feelings of relief about the suicide are common when the relationship was superficial or destructive. Now that the cause of their emotional turmoil is gone, many family members breathe silent sighs of relief after the suicide. Often, an unspoken death wish had been felt toward the deceased, and the actual event fulfills this unconscious desire. When relief, rather than grief, follows suicide, people often bypass the emotional flood that follows shock.

Catharsis

A Greek word meaning "purging" or "purification," catharsis follows shock in most grief experiences. In this phase, the numbness begins to wear off and you realize the great loss that has occurred in your life. This emotional flood feels uncontrollable. You feel swept away by overpowering emotions. These feelings tend to peak at the funeral, and they will usually be quite strong for another week or two. You might well be reading this during your own period of catharsis.

Here is some of what you can expect during this phase of grief. When one emotion is let loose, others will soon follow. You'll feel floods of fear, denial, guilt, anger, relief, and depression all at once—an emotional mob scene. This is normal: most suicide survivors are more "emotional" than those experiencing normal grief. What may seem abnormal or "hysterical" to you is actually quite natural for people in your situation. Remember, you need to let these feelings come out. If you don't let them out *now*, they'll come out some other time, some other way. *That* you can count on. You won't suffer nearly as much from "getting too upset" as you will from "being brave" and keeping your honest emotions all locked up inside.

During this experience of emotional release, you'll have to deal with two crucial questions: whether to admit that the death was a suicide, and whom to tell about it. How you answer these questions can determine the course of your later mourning. By this time, the word *will* be out, and your decisions can help or hinder your "grief work" in the days ahead.

Let me add one further word. None of your emotions is forbidden. If you feel something, express it! I agree with Elisabeth Kübler-Ross's suggestion that you find a "screaming room" where you can "let your hair down" and "come unglued." Coming unglued can be healthy and honestly good for you, especially if the "glue" was a mixture of repression and denial. I recommend that you share your "ungluedness" with supportive loved ones, as often as you feel the need.

DEPRESSION

Catharsis is a gut-wrenching experience. It will drain you until fatigue and sleep take over. When you've gotten it all out, and cried your eyes dry, depression comes with the realization that this thing really *did* happen, that your loved one really *is* dead. Others who have survived suicide, who understand what you're going through, say that this depressed feeling will last for about six months.

Every person has a different experience with depression. Some withdraw and isolate themselves, and get stuck there for months or years. They feel that suicide has ruled out any hope of something better for them. It may happen that you will even contemplate suicide yourself during this time. Many do, especially after the third month or so, when they hit rock bottom. I urge you to get help if you start feeling that way. You're not losing your mind—you're reacting to the blow of a terrible emotional injury, and you *can* be helped.

A major concern during this depressed period will be your health. Don't be surprised if you don't feel well physically during this time. Other survivors report hundreds of physical symptoms that appeared in the weeks and months following the suicide. These begin during the stage of shock, with complaints like those about which you read above. Survivors complain about things like nervousness and fatigue, general tiredness, breaking out in rashes and hives, distorted vision, upset stomachs and spastic colons; even the symptoms of asthma and rheumatoid arthritis appear in the aftershock of suicide. Women report menstrual difficulty as common among their physical problems. In fact, well over half of the suicide spouses in one study said that they were sick more often after the suicide than before.

Of course, you need to see your doctor if you begin to feel poorly. Acute grief can often give its warning signs through the symptoms of quite serious illnesses. Most likely, however, your physician will tell you that your symptoms are "psychosomatic" or will give you a prescription for your "nerves." You need to know what that means and whether such treatment is for you.

The word "psychosomatic" is not a medical put-down. Your doctor doesn't mean that you're only imagining this illness. You are *not* a hypochondriac. A psychosomatic symptom is a physical problem brought on by an emotional reaction. It is *real.* You really feel the pain and distress because it is really happening. Just as normal stress and strain may bring on a tension headache or "butterflies" in an upset stomach, the heavy shock of suicide can also result in more intense physical reactions.

Beware of simplistic medical treatment at this point. Most of us tend to be like sheep before a physician, especially when we're grief-stricken. Remember, M.D. stands for Medical Doctor, not Minor Deity! Drugs may certainly serve a purpose in your situation, but they won't cure your grief. In fact, they may complicate the healing process as much as they aid it. If your doctor gives you a "nerve pill," ask for which "nerve" it is intended! What you're getting is most likely a tranquilizer, like Valium, to sedate you and make you groggy.

I agree with those physicians and counselors who believe that grief is handled best when you're *awake,* not drugged into sleepiness. Tranquilizers won't end the pain. They'll only mask it for a while. Unless your symptoms are so severe that drugs are medically required, I urge you to resist zonking yourself out during this period. Grief work is done best when you are alert, not off on a medicated cloud.

GUILT

When the shock of suicide first hit you, you began to ask questions such as: What did I do to cause this? Could I have prevented it? Is this my fault? Feelings of guilt are common in all grief, but they're compounded among suicide survivors. Guilt is the focus of *the* dramatic difference in the grief of suicide and nonsuicide survivors. The great majority of people who have grieved over suicide indicate that their grief was complicated by massive guilt feelings. And, for some, the guilt never goes away. Either they let it ruin their lives, or they allow it to diminish to the point where they can handle it.

After the flood of emotions is past, the deep, haunting feelings of guilt really set in. You begin to deal with the primary question of *responsibility*—of whose fault it was, and who is to blame. Our society tends to teach us that suicide is always caused by *problems.* The death wasn't accidental; it wasn't beyond control. When it happens, you start questioning whether the problem in this instance was yourself.

Guilt comes in many forms, wearing many disguises. You may feel guilty for the conscious or unconscious death wishes you had toward the deceased—the "I wish he'd do it and get it over with" feeling. You start to relive all the angry words and harsh encounters you had, dwelling on how bad they were and how much to blame you were. You think about how much more you could have done for the deceased. If you had an argument shortly before the suicide, you blame yourself for directly causing the death. If you express anger over the suicide, you feel guilty for being angry at a dead person. If you only feel relief, then you feel guilty for *not* feeling guilty. Either way you look at it, you can lose. If you try hard enough, you can replay the fourth quarter so that the loss is always on your shoulders.

The most serious guilt feelings come to spouses of suicides. Here the entire marriage is held up for public examination. The survivor imagines that others see the suicide as proof that she was a failure as a spouse. Unspoken questions are raised: Why didn't someone report those earlier attempts? Why didn't you force him to get help? How could you let him leave the hospital in that condition? Why didn't you do something to prevent it? Feelings of shame, failure, unworthiness, and hopelessness wash over the surviving spouse. One woman told me that she felt like a leper in first-century Jerusalem, forced to cry "Unclean! Unclean!" wherever she went.

How do you deal with your severe feelings of guilt? How do you respond to those who you feel are all pointing their fingers at you? Moreover, how can you keep from constantly blaming yourself?

One way of response is through *denial.* You can convince yourself that the death was an accident or a homicide, and thereby remove the question of your responsibility from the situation. I hear this approach from parents of adolescents who "accidentally" overdosed on an entire bottle of sleeping pills or "accidentally" shot themselves in the head. Another case, reported by Peter Whitis, involved a thirteen-year-old boy who hanged or strangled himself while the family was away from home. The boy's father reacted by denying that the death had been a suicide. Whitis describes this denial for us: "When he could no longer get the police to investigate, he began his own investigation and still remained convinced that 'foul play' was involved. For him, the explanation of the death was still open. 'Someday, someone will come forth with what happened' " (Peter R. Whitis, "The Legacy of a Child's Suicide," in Cain, ed., *Survivors of Suicide,* p. 159).

Blaming others for the suicide will also help suppress guilt for a while. "It was God's will" is often heard from those who want to blame God for the death and relieve themselves of any responsibility. Blame is leveled at any of a number of persons who had a role in the deceased's emotional distress: parents, psychiatrists, employers, sexual partners, and others.

The suicide can be *rationalized.* Here one looks for reasons or causes onto which responsibility for the death can be placed. Mental illness is often mentioned, as are alcoholism and drug addiction. Though these problems can certainly play important roles in a suicidal crisis, and even lead a person to attempt suicide while hallucinating, they can't bear the tremendous weight of having all your guilt dumped upon them. These rationalizations probably won't rid you of your guilt; they'll only veil it from view for a while.

I believe that guilt can be most helpfully managed through the religious practices of confession and forgiveness. This requires, first of all, that you honestly face up to what has happened to your family and to your role in that crisis. You can't go back and undo anything now. It's done, and you won't really live in peace until you *accept* what you already know.

Confession means self-revelation. You need to throw open the windows of your soul and "tell the whole truth and nothing but the truth" about what is making you feel guilty. You can make this confession to God in secret, and you can make it to a trusted professional in confidence. Tell the honest truth about yourself, and your outside and your insides will begin to come together. Your minister should be willing to assist you in your confessing.

The church has found its message of liberation in the *forgiveness* and mercy of God. We know that forgiveness comes freely from God, that we can't earn it, and that it's never withdrawn from us. Paul Tillich called it "being ac-

cepted" by God. The Baptists of my heritage mean the same
thing when they sing the old gospel song "Just as I Am." The
liberating forgiveness of God and of your fellow human beings "restoreth the soul," and helps you share the load of the
baggage of guilt you carry. God's forgiveness has a beautiful
added advantage: it enables you to begin to forgive yourself.
As Paul put it so simply, "If God is for us, who is against us?"
(Rom. 8:31).

The blessed therapy of *restitution* follows forgiveness but
is never a precondition for it. You can't bribe God into
forgiving you. He's not "taking." Restitution is *your* opportunity to restore the loving relationships between you and your
family. You can make amends for some of your past mistakes.
Your life is able to change for the better. You can ensure that
what you're going through now will not happen again. One
woman in her thirties found this process to be a positive force
in her life as she got busy with this business of restitution.

> It makes you a better person, because you stop and think twice
> before you scream at someone . . . because you think twice
> before saying something, because words can never be taken
> back, and I think now before I say something terribly unkind
> in anger . . . *Guilt is marvelous, because you can reverse it and
> make it work for you.* (In Stone, *Suicide and Grief,* p. 87)

A competent, compassionate therapist can help you repair
your feelings toward the deceased. The things you still want
to say to the dead person can be said. With professional counsel
you can express all your feelings about what happened. Take
this opportunity to say good-by. Say all the things that the
suicide prevented you from saying. Remember the good times
you had together. You can "free up" guilt this way, and avoid

getting stuck in it. Try focusing on this guilt, giving it a shape and a color. When you can do this and make it tangible, you regain control over your life and free yourself from guilt's often destructive power. You can transform it by changing your past mistakes into a new life-style for the future.

Preoccupation with the Loss

During your time of depression, you will find many of your waking moments to be dominated by thoughts of the suicide. This is a normal occurrence in grief. It appears in a variety of ways. Many of these emotional reactions are harmless, and to be expected. Others are potentially destructive. All your alertness will be needed to avoid getting stuck in this phase of grief. I share with you here some facets of preoccupation as a road map for the way ahead.

Daydreaming. Fantasizing about the death is common and should not be of concern to you. You'll find yourself pretending that it didn't happen, that you were able to prevent it, and that soon everything will be back to normal. Another common fantasy is that the person is just away on a trip, soon to return safe and sound. Such daydreams are emotional breathers, and may help you keep your balance when your feelings are getting overloaded. They will fade in time, as long as you don't dwell on them and retreat into a dream world.

Identification. Survivors often unconsciously mimic the lost family member, adopting his mannerisms or tone of voice. This isn't particularly unusual: we usually pick up similar habits and peculiarities from many people who are close to us. However, it can be destructive if it turns into a rigid denial of the death. I happen to think this *can* be a helpful way of keeping in touch with cherished memories, as long as you don't overdo it and get stuck here. Think of it as a way to "incarnate" the things about the deceased that are precious to you.

Bereavement Dreams. You've probably already awakened in tears several times as you relived the suicide and your period of shock and catharsis. These dreams are quite normal. They will subside in time, and should not alarm you. They *will* show you a lot about yourself, often allowing you to express feelings that you're unwilling to admit to yourself while awake. As Wayne Oates points out, the bereavement dream helps you "renegotiate" your life on the emotional levels that exist beneath the surface (Oates, *Pastoral Care and Counseling in Grief and Separation,* p. 44).

Shrine-building. This drive toward creating a "museum to the deceased" is one way to ensure a lifetime of grief. Visiting the grave every day may be helpful for a while, but it can soon become your method of refusing to let go. I know families who have had color photographs of the deceased embedded in the granite gravestone. I've seen them place ornate benches at the grave for their daily visits. For many families, visiting the grave becomes an after-church ritual each Sunday for years and years. One man reportedly visited his wife's grave every day until his own death. In the meantime, he remarried and was subsequently divorced by his second wife, who wouldn't join him in his daily vigil.

Another method of shrine-building is the preservation of a room in the house "just like it was when he died." Clothes are kept in the closet. Furniture is never moved. The walls are lined with photographs and mementos of the deceased. Dean Schuyler tells of a couple who bought a new house soon after the suicide of their son. The mother insisted that a bedroom be set aside in the new house as a shrine to her child! (Dean Schuyler, "Counseling Suicide Survivors: Issues and Answers," *Omega*, Vol. 4, Winter 1973, p. 318.) This is "frozen" grief. It promises a lifetime of mourning for those who succumb to its nostalgic temptations.

Rabbi Earl Grollman makes some helpful suggestions about this tendency. He suggests that you resist the compulsion to create a memorial shrine by (1) giving away the clothes of the deceased and (2) rearranging the furniture of the bedroom, and perhaps even the entire house (Earl Grollman, *Talking About Death: A Dialogue Between Parent and Child*, p. 69; new ed., Beacon Press, 1976). Donate the clothes to the Salvation Army or Goodwill Industries, *not* to a neighbor, close friend, or other family member: you don't need to see the clothes being worn by someone you know. Move the furniture so that it creates new traffic patterns in the house. This will help you combat the fantasies of "seeing" the deceased in familiar places in the home. Grollman cautions against throwing away your photographs and mementos. You don't want to make a shrine out of them, but you also don't want to repudiate the memories they represent. My rule of thumb, which I'll add to Grollman's suggestions, is: *keep* what you must have to live, *give* to friends or family what you treasure but can't live with, and *donate* to charity what you can live without.

A touchy issue must be discussed here. You will have to decide what to do with the suicide note, if one was left behind. This has the potential to be a major source of hurt and disappointment for you in the future. Talk about it with your family before you do anything, but face this question *soon.* Don't let this note rattle around your dresser drawer for ten years of indecision. If you think it will only bring you pain, then have a private, symbolic burning, and commit its contents to the memory of God.

Selective Memory. You will have flashbacks of the deceased and the suicide from time to time. Even though your life will return to some degree of normalcy, something will happen to trigger what Oates calls "selective memory." You'll see someone who resembles your family member, hear a favorite song, smell a cologne or tobacco used by him, or see someone driving the same color and model car. When this happens, you "flash back" into a kind of mini-grief that can last for several days. These feelings of overwhelming sadness may surprise you with their intensity. You'll wonder where they were hidden. The answer lies in your *memory:* it is readjusting, and that takes time. Oates describes this phenomenon:

> These periods of reflectiveness and heavyheartedness tend to become less frequent with the passage of time, and for a reason. *Each person, place, thing, activity, event, item on the daily agenda of a person's life must eventually be associated with the present reality: "My loved one is dead."* These items are innumerable to begin with, but their number is gradually whittled down as day by day they are associated with new realities in one's present life. As this happens, habits of thought and behavior are being reconditioned. (Oates, *Pastoral Care and Counseling in Grief and Separation,* pp. 43–44; emphasis added)

In other words, your mind and emotions are "retooling" for the remainder of your life ahead.

Idealization. No hard and fast deductions can be made about the idolatry of the dead by their survivors. Families idealize everyone from beautiful young children to hardened old reprobates, and for vastly different reasons. I have seen a wife swear out a warrant for her husband's arrest one week and then mourn him as a "saint of God" after his tragic death the next. Suicide tends to minimize this tendency, for the manner of death is not "heroic." Yet, idealization of the suicide still occurs, and it blocks healthy grieving with yet another obstacle. In many instances, people think of the deceased as some sort of god! They make this lost family member the center and focus of their entire lives. This is really a more entrenched form of denial. The family members decide to think only good thoughts about the deceased, and they make him a martyr in their sight.

Preoccupation, as you have seen, doesn't have to be destructive. As you recall again and again the stored-away memories of your loved one, as you remember the suicide and your reaction to it, this repetition will help you work through your feelings of loss and sorrow. Gradually your "unfinished business" will be completed and your memory will heal as well.

ANGER

Although your feelings of rage may be tumultuous for you and those around you, they represent something positively healthy. Anger shows that you're coming out from the depths of depression. You can express your feelings again, without fear. Getting that anger out should be one of your major goals in your process of "postvention."

It seems silly to discuss whether or not you have a right to be angry, and it is. That kind of question ignores the rage you feel inside. It ignores pent-up emotions that aren't labeled "right" or "wrong," "good" or "bad." Others like yourself report a great deal of anger in the months after suicide. You may feel terribly guilty for those feelings, but you need to know that it's perfectly O.K. for you to express them. You do indeed have that right.

From what memories does all this anger come after suicide? What causes the rage to boil over? Several factors come readily to mind.

1. Survivors feel rage toward the deceased for publicly rejecting them. Suicide is a form of desertion, a way of saying "I abandon you" for all to see. Anger is your natural response to such treatment. When we're treated so unfairly, we usually do "get mad." Wives, husbands, mothers, and fathers often find themselves furious after the suicide has left them to be full-time mourners with a life full of responsibilities.

2. Anger often arises over the lasting effects of the death. When suicide is used as a last, ultimate weapon against loved ones, it is usually successful. As Howard Stone says, "Suicide works!" People are devastated at its result. As you begin to realize the long-range effects of the act, you too may find yourself shaking with rage over the one who "did this to you."

3. Many people respond to suicide by shaking their fist at God, usually through a nearby minister, rabbi, or priest. Here the survivor is raging at God for singling him out for special punishment. He screams, "Why did you do this to me?" as though every minute action in the universe was directly willed by some kind of deterministic deity. As I say at greater length in Chapter 5, God is the only one prepared to handle *all* your anger at him. If you're ticked off at the Almighty, for his sake tell him!

4. Anger is directed toward others. It's easy to get into a "me against the world" mentality after suicide. If you can find just one person on whom you can unload for what he "did" to your family member, you may not be able to resist giving him hell for his transgressions. What this amounts to is a convenient form of denial. If you can project your rage on everyone else, you may not have to aim it at the deceased. And you may be able to escape it yourself.

5. Survivors get angry with themselves for what they did or didn't do to change the destructive course of events that led to suicide. But this is different from guilt. *This* anger goes farther, so that you decide to punish yourself through self-destructive acts. This is one type of anger that you should obviously refrain from expressing physically. Cutting *your* wrists or drowning yourself won't solve anything and may well demolish your already crippled family.

All your hostility needs to come out. Yelling and screaming is one way to ventilate it. Tearing towels, punching pillows, and chopping wood are also recommended. I even think that hauling off and "cussing a blue streak" is beneficial if it will help you through this difficult period of acute grief. Express your rage without feeling guilty. In other words, you can be angry with confidence! As Paul advised the church at Ephesus, "Be angry and do not sin; do not let the sun go down on your anger" (Eph. 4:26). In other words, burn your fire and put it out; smoldering coals are dangerous to everybody.

We have seen the complex of strong emotions felt by suicide survivors. Sometimes you feel like the man whom Jesus met in a graveyard, a man so torn by inner conflict that when Jesus asked him his name, he replied "My name is

Legion; for we are many" (Mark 5:9). Robert Raines, in his sermon "My Name is Mob," speaks to this feeling of inner chaos which comes to survivors.

> I keep hoping that there is some way that the manyness of me may be released into a unity that can thrive wisely.
>
> What about you? How is it with you and your many you's and your longing to be a single person? A man writes, "I believe that everything wants a living place—its home, if you will, where it becomes what its essence is at a certain time and in a certain place. For example, a man who rests his case for life upon a sounding place, a spot on which his life can stand and from which he can say, 'Here the trembling stops.' "
>
> Where does the trembling stop for you? With whom? Treasure those moments, rare perhaps, moments of peace, silent wonder, communion, joy. Moments, times, places where for you the trembling stops. Moments when the mob in you becomes a community. Moments when you are quiet, together. Like maybe . . . now. (Robert Raines, *To Kiss the Joy*, p. 108; Word Books, 1973)

My prayer for you in this time is that as we journey together through this "extended letter" of a book, your trembling might be stilled and your life might begin to return to wholeness. You are a survivor! The trembling is subsiding . . .

3. A Family of Survivors

Suicide is a singular act with a plural effect. One person's act of suicide can throw hundreds of others into shock and grief. If the person is a public figure—a Marilyn Monroe or Freddie Prinze, for example—thousands are affected. When the suicide bomb drops, however, one group of people is always standing at ground zero: the members of the surviving family. You are the ones who are shocked and stigmatized by the death. You feel the deepest rejection. That's why you are the hurting ones to whom this book is written. *You* have *survived* a death by suicide. As Arnold Toynbee says so clearly, "death's sting is two-pronged . . . and, in the apportionment of the suffering, the survivor takes the brunt" (Arnold Toynbee, "The Relation Between Life and Death, Living and Dying," in Edwin S. Shneidman, ed., *Death: Current Perspectives*, pp. 330, 332; Mayfield Publishing Co., 1976). This is your book for dealing with that sting.

This chapter aims to help your family pull together and stay that way in the weeks and months of the aftershock. Each of you will be tempted to withdraw into your individual shell and mourn alone. The jealousies and hard feelings that existed before the suicide will remain. They may even be inflamed by the death. You need to step back *now* and take a long look at this family of yours, while you still can. You see, suicide throws a triple whammy on all of you. In the first place, you've lost an immediate family member. This brings a normal amount of grief for you. Secondly, you've experienced the pain and shock of a sudden death. On top of all that, you have to deal with the fact of suicide, with its additional pain and regret. No family is strong enough to ignore that triple shock. As Bettie Arthur says, suicide isn't just another family crisis, "it's a violent force slamming into what had been the relatively stable . . . family relationship, and one that may produce seemingly unending reverberations within the structure" (Bettie Arthur, "Parent Suicide: A Family Affair," in Cain, ed., *Survivors of Suicide,* p. 257).

Yet there are some constructive steps that can be taken. I want to help your family start on the path toward healing and permanent "survival." My prayer is that this constant reminder of violence in your midst can give way to a new and lasting peace that passes all understanding.

GAMES FAMILIES PLAY

In his landmark book *Games People Play* (Grove Press, 1964), Eric Berne popularized the concept of psychological "games." He defined a game as an ulterior behavior pattern that usually involves some kind of "con." These patterns are usually destructive, motivated by hidden desires to win a payoff of some kind or a desired feeling. Berne believed that you and I learn these games in our childhood and then play them throughout our lives. Each of us has our own personal repertoire of games. We base our relationships on finding other people who want to play the game with us.

Families play games together just as you and I do individu-
ally. We have seen that suicide doesn't happen in a vacuum.
It drops like a bomb into a real, relating family. It kicks off
an incredible round of negative family games that can become destructive if they're not adequately refereed. I have
listed ten of the most common games played by families in
the aftermath of suicide. If you can recognize them as currently part of your family's grief process, you can take steps
to end them and keep your family together.

Scapegoating. The ancient Hebrew ritual of atonement
involved an annual observance in which a live goat was driven
out into the wilderness, symbolically laden with the sins of the
people (Lev. 16:9–10). From this image we derive the term
"scapegoat" to refer to a person who bears blame for others.

Dean Schuyler has pointed out the tremendous amounts of
time and energy used by family members who will not rest
until blame has been assigned for the suicide (Dean Schuyler,
"Counseling Suicide Survivors: Issues and Answers," p. 316).
In this game, finger-pointing is the favorite activity and "she
drove him to it" is the motto. Sometimes blame is directed
outward, toward anyone thought to have a role in the death.
But scapegoating takes its most destructive form when it
throws a family into blaming each other. Those who play this
game can only ease their feelings of guilt by blaming someone
else, and so a vicious circle of scapegoating begins. This game
can turn into real tragedy when all the family members gang
up on one or two other relatives. The victims are helpless
against the crowd. In this game, no one really wins. When
relatives turn on each other in this way, the whole family
loses.

Keeping an Impossible Secret. The stigma that suicide
causes is more than some families can bear. They would
rather actively attempt to cover up the fact of suicide, or
adopt an attitude of "we know but we're not telling." Families get a lot of help in this camouflage from sympathetic
doctors, reporters, coroners, and police. James Wechsler, in
his book about the mental illness and suicide of his son,
describes how the police and a reporter offered to keep under
wraps the details about the suicide. "Even in the numbness
of those hours, we were astonished at the prevalence of the
view that suicide was a dishonorable or at least disreputable
matter, to be charitably covered up to protect Michael's good
name and the sensibilities of the family" (James A. Wechsler,
In a Darkness, W. W. Norton & Co., 1972; quoted in Louise
Klagsbrun, *Too Young to Die: Youth and Suicide,* p. 100;
Pocket Books, 1977). You can see why suicide statistics are
so inaccurate! This negative game becomes even more serious
when family members go to extremes. They will destroy suicide notes, hide crucial evidence from the police and the
coroner, and bribe or pressure officials to list the death officially as an accident.

This game is also destined for failure. People do find out
about the suicide and then watch in embarrassment as family
members gamely pretend that everything is normal. It makes
for loneliness and isolation for the family, and again, no one
wins.

The Survival Myth. This game is similar to Keeping an
Impossible Secret, with one difference: in this game, family
members themselves refuse to accept the fact of death by
suicide. Even in the face of solid evidence, they choose to
keep alive the possibility of accidental death or murder. For

these "players," suicide "just can't be."

This denial is greatest when the family has lost a child. In one case, mentioned earlier, a family returned home to find that their adolescent son had hanged himself in the garage. In spite of solid evidence to that effect, the father steadfastly refused to accept the death as suicide, insisting that foul play had occurred. He launched his own investigation and invested much time and money to prove the police wrong. He never succeeded. What he did do was to retard his own grief and get himself out of sync with the rest of his family (Peter Whitis, "The Legacy of a Child's Suicide," in Cain, ed., *Survivors of Suicide,* p. 159).

A common element of this game is the use of the language of "normal" grief in place of phrases like "killed himself," "took his own life," and "committed suicide."

Circle the Wagons. This game is a variation on both The Survival Myth and Keeping an Impossible Secret. Like the pioneer caravan in hostile territory, the family draws together in a defensive pattern. It becomes "us against them." The group feels threatened by rejection and stigmatizing by others. They develop a "family resistance system" that acts as a barrier against communication with those outside the family. Turning inward, they project a great deal of anger onto society. Newspapers become "the enemy," for they report the suicide and make private problems public. Coroners are railed against for scheduling an inquest and autopsy. Insurance companies feel the family's wrath when they raise questions about the claim. Attending physicians, especially psychiatrists, literally catch hell for not preventing the suicide or for "making" the person suicidal through the prescribing of certain medications.

This game can be partially valuable—at least the family members aren't blaming and bickering with each other. Their solidarity may make them a closer family, even if it alienates everyone else. However, the game remains destructive, for it is only a form of denial. And the loneliness that comes from making everyone else an "enemy" can turn into lifelong isolation. This is a form of social suicide.

King (or Queen) of the Mountain. When a parent completes suicide, especially the father or a single parent, this game is likely to go into effect. In this pattern, family members jostle for leadership and power. You can imagine how this works when the family is wealthy or owns its own business. As Eli Marcovitz points out, each family member approaches this game from his or her own self-interest. In other words, each relative asks, "How is this going to affect *me* now and in the future?" (Eli Marcovitz, "What Is the Meaning of Death to the Dying Person and His Survivors?" *Omega,* Vol. 4, Spring 1973, p. 19). This kind of attitude among all the members can make a family disintegrate in short order. As each operates from the principle of "What's in it for me?" the family as a whole gets lost in the shuffle.

As the new family leader emerges from this free-for-all, the anger begins to surface from the losers. Younger children may be seriously hurt when an older child becomes the new "man (or woman) of the house." The conniving spirit at work results in a win-lose situation for everyone, and only one can win.

The Silent Treatment. Cain and Fast call this family game a "conspiracy of silence" (Albert Cain and Irene Fast, "The Legacy of Suicide: Observations on the Pathogenic Impact of Suicide upon Marital Partners," in Cain, ed., *Survivors of*

Suicide, p. 149). It's a kind of "cold war" where most communication is cut off. Family members don't talk to each other. They don't touch. Each grieves alone, behind closed doors. They avoid each other's gaze, raising their eyes or staring down at the ground in passing. This can be the most devastating game in the book. Such silence has at least these negative effects on the family. (1) It keeps helpful grief work from happening within the whole group. (2) It stifles catharsis, the outpouring of emotions in normal grief. (3) It limits the opportunity for each member to check out his or her fears and fantasies with those of the other members. (4) It allows misconceptions and wrong information to flourish, since one's own view of what happened is never tested. (5) It lets guilt and anger rage on quietly, with no hope for resolving the problems that are hurting each person.

Who Loved/Was Loved the Most? Some family members will fight each other for the coveted title of "Most Loved by the Deceased." "She was her favorite" is music to their ears. Likewise, they'll argue at length to prove that *they* are the ones who have suffered the greatest loss, who always went the second mile for the deceased, and who loved her the best. Why all this futile arguing? Several reasons can explain it. It can be someone's ticket to family leadership and power. It can be someone else's way of overcoming guilt and self-blame for *not* really loving the deceased very much. It's a way to get even with those members who "never gave a damn."

This game has a flip side, played when the deceased was the source of much trouble within the family. This side, called "Who Was Treated the Worst?" is designed to gain sympathy from other family members. If the deceased was really hateful, then the person who received the most abuse can

gain quite an advantage over others on the basis of their pity
and guilt.

Let's Grieve Forever. This game involves a perpetual state
of mourning. I call it the "black armband" reaction. Family
members wear their grief as a badge for all to see, and they
do it without end. All this is seen as the only loving way to
grieve over the deceased; anything less would be evidence of
selfishness and lack of devotion. Widows swear on their husbands' graves never to remarry. Daily trips are planned to the
cemetery. Shrines are created in the deceased's bedroom.
Laughter is outlawed. Pained expressions are required.

This extended mourning is primarily an attempt to allevi-
ate guilt, to make up for shortcomings in life and death.
Parents of young children have an especially hard time here.
They continue to see their child as "needing Mommy and
Daddy," and they feel guilty because they can't be of any
help. Families often get stuck in this kind of eternal grief to
the extent that they are never able to bring it to a close in
any respectable way. Life for them cannot go on without the
deceased. Eternal bereavement is their way of "freezing the
action."

Halo and Pitchfork. The halo placed over the suicide's life
is the result of what psychiatrists call *idealization.* In the Halo
game, only good things are allowed to be remembered about
the deceased. All the details of the stormy relationships that
existed in the family are hushed up. The suicide is often seen
as a brave act of courage, a "noble gesture."

All the previous feelings of anger and frustration are re-
placed with beautiful memories of steadfast love. Small children often express this "halo effect" by *identifying* with the
deceased. Hajal described a little girl whose father completed

suicide. The child began to remark again and again about how much she looked like her father and how they had liked and disliked the same things. At the same time, she became very critical of her mother in order to justify this comparison (Fady Hajal, "Post-Suicide Grief Work in Family Therapy," *Journal of Marriage and Family Counseling,* Vol. 3, April 1977, pp. 37–39).

The Pitchfork game works the same way, but with opposite intentions. Here the members come not to praise the deceased, but to bury him or her with insults and recriminations. Anger, hurt feelings, betrayal—all are projected onto the suicide without mercy. Families talk of the burdens the person created, the problems that arose, and what a "devil" the suicide was. The suicidal act is interpreted as an act of revenge, punishment, or cowardice. Feelings of desertion and abandonment run high. In general, players of this game go to extremes in denying the significance and worth of the deceased.

Both sections of this game are examples of defensive reactions used by families when their gut-level emotional responses threaten to overwhelm them. The Halo game shuts off anger and resentment. The Pitchfork game stifles guilt, hurt feelings, and love. But neither of these games "works" forever. Sooner or later those emotions will surface, and the catch-up grieving may last far longer than a normal, healthy grief.

Head for the Hills. Running away is the point of this game. Here families pack up and move away from the "suicide house," usually within one year after the death. This is especially prevalent when the suicide actually happened in the house or on the family property. These players can't walk past the spot without cringing in horror. They "see" the deceased everywhere, "hear" his footsteps, and have nightmares about the suicide happening again. So, they get out. They exchange one set of problems for a brand-new batch.

In her moving story, *Widow,* Lynn Caine described the trauma of moving with her children, after the death of her husband, from their home in Manhattan into a suburban house in New Jersey.

Most of my ridiculous actions—asking a politician I had met once for half a million dollars, trying to revive a love affair that was eighteen years dead—these were all minor craziness. They pale in the face of other insanities I committed. The major one was moving.

Within three months after Martin died, I had given up our comfortable apartment in Manhattan, bought a house I hated across the river in Hackensack, New Jersey, pulled the children out of their New York schools and enrolled them in new suburban schools, embraced a way of life that did not appeal to me, that I was not suited for, could not afford and could not cope with. I was absolutely irresponsible and crazy. And even today I can't explain what was going through my head. . . .

I had really believed that the move would be good for the children. And it *was* in some ways. They had a certain physical freedom they didn't have in the city. But they were isolated, too. From me. The one important fact that I did not take into consideration was that nothing could be good for the children if it was not good for me. Our emotional and physical well-being is so closely interlocked that I must be healthy and functioning (and that adds up to happy) if I am to be able to give them the love and time and support they deserve and need. And they did not get it. They were not getting enough love in that year I spent in the hell that Hackensack represented for me, because I did not have enough to give. I tried. Yes, I did. But I failed. I was too crazy, too sad, too lonely.

(Lynn Caine, *Widow*, pp. 107, 113; William Morrow & Co., 1974).

Moving to avoid the grim memories of suicide and "those who know" is not always this destructive. If you live in the middle of a community of finger pointers, then getting away may be the best thing for your family. I only caution you to make sure of what it is you're fleeing. You can't ever run far or fast enough to escape the memory of the suicide. Somewhere you'll have to take your stand.

SURVIVING TOGETHER

The destructive games mentioned in this chapter operate with a common denominator. That is, most of the families who play these games have blocked off all effective communication among themselves. If they could all sit down together just once, to cry, rage, and feel guilty *together*, they could build a foundation of support that might prevent the games from ever being played. Communication is the key to surviving *together* in the aftermath of suicide. It occurs in your family in two different forms.

Verbal communication involves speaking and *listening*, not just speaking and hearing. Active listening on your part can make a difference in the way your family gets along in the months ahead. Here are some hints on how to make healthy verbal communication work for you and your loved ones.

1. Be sensitive to how others feel. Communication depends more on feelings than on facts. So, resist the urge to prove your point at all costs. Your ego may feel better, but your family relationships will be seriously harmed.

2. Listen not only to what the other persons say but also to who they are. In other words, respond to your children in ways important to them, even though their desires seem insignificant to you.

3. Pay attention to your family members when you're with them. Save your daydreaming and fantasizing for some other time. Give your undivided attention to whomever you are with.

4. Listen to what is being said. Remember, we often send two or three messages when we talk to each other. Be sure you hear what is being meant as well as what is being spoken.

5. Open your heart to the other person. Honesty has no substitutes. However, it does have a partner, known as *acceptance.* Be willing to accept what the other person honestly shares with you. That doesn't mean that you must agree with what the person says. It does require that you agree with who they are.

6. Let others *be* around you. Be careful not to so dominate things that others are left out. If you're a compulsive talker, or the pushy type, learn the value of sitting back and listening to what others are saying.

Not all communication is verbal, as we have seen. Families who don't touch are also sending messages. *Nonverbal communication* is transmitted through the senses of sight, smell, and touch. When family members declare a cold war on closeness, communication is just as blocked as if they weren't speaking. Many of the things that your family needs to communicate cannot be put into words. How can you talk about a hug, for instance?

Sometimes a comfortable silence is the answer to the deep hurts of a family. The difference between such a silence and the deep freeze of The Silent Treatment is dramatic, because here you are able to communicate through touch and "silent eyes." You can help cultivate this kind of communication in your family by doing it yourself. Try "saying" things without speaking, as a start.

IF YOUR FAMILY NEEDS A COUNSELOR

Our country is full of families in transition—those who have been shocked and transformed by divorce, death, and numerous other causes. Although each individual person in your family has problems in such a situation as suicide, the entire family also suffers as a group. The group will occasionally need guidance itself. The members of the family feel the need for leadership as they try to cope together. The family is a powerful system of relationships. When it is troubled, it needs help.

Family counseling focuses on the group in just this way, instead of attempting to help each individual person in isolation from the rest of the group. This is not to say that individual counseling is unnecessary. Rather, just the reverse is true. Individual counseling is probably the rule in suicide grief. But in those situations where the entire family needs help in its relationships, family counseling can be a beacon in the darkness.

Family counseling recognizes that problems *between* persons can be just as serious as problems *within* persons. If your family finds itself in a destructive pattern of game-playing following suicide, then you might consider getting some help for the group. Family counselors will meet with all family members together, to observe how you relate to each other and where communication is being blocked. They can sit back and see things that you're too close to see. Many competent and professionally trained family counselors are at work today with countless "families in transition."

Local health services across the country are also taking the lead in providing family counseling for the suicide survivors in their areas. Several county programs in California are attracting widespread attention. A joint program of the San Diego County Health Services and Coroner's Office, in existence since 1971, brings suicide survivors together monthly to share their experiences. The sessions encourage emotional release and help the families move toward readjustment to healthy living. Practical problems like settling insurance claims and moving to a less expensive home are discussed. Group members are free to raise any question. Those who have participated in these sessions report that the experience helped them on the path to emotional healing.

Another program of family "postvention" is under way at the San Bernardino County Department of Public Health. Known as the Suicide Survivor Follow-up Program, its first purpose is to provide an atmosphere of support and comfort for the families of suicide victims. Lately, this program has been expanded to offer help for friends, employers, and other related survivors of the shock of suicide. The directors hope that the process of working through the difficult suicide grief will bring quicker recovery to emotional balance for all involved. The hush-hush attitude among families begins to fade as they are able to bring their feelings and problems out into the open.

These programs and others like them are lifesavers. They need to be studied and reproduced in every part of the country. Churches should take the lead. In smaller cities and rural areas, where the suicide rate is lower and more manageable, churches can organize programs of "postvention" for survivors of suicide and other traumatic deaths. What better place to find help than an intimate community of dedicated caregivers in a church! My hope is that churches and synagogues across America will begin to take seriously their positions as the front line of defense against emotional distress and unhealthy grief. They can move rapidly to begin the process of healing and recovery. I hope you can either find or help begin such a support group to breathe into your family the breath of life and hope that you need right now.

Your work within your family will be your most challenging task in the months ahead. This includes your own grief work, since you must be "together" yourself in order to help your family toward togetherness. I can't promise you instant success, or even freedom from pain. As I mentioned before, you've been hit with a triple whammy, which makes your grief last three times as long. Yet you can all become a family of survivors if you keep the channels of love and communication open. Talk to each other! Touch each other at every opportunity! Weep together, rage together, keep silence together. In the midst of your grief you can seize the hope that God has set before you.

Let me share an afterthought with you. The word "survive" comes from two Latin words: *super,* which means "over," and *vivere,* which means "to live." Do you catch the wealth of meaning in this word? As a survivor, you have a chance to start over, to continue a life that you felt might well be over. You can "live over"; you can *live* again. Your family is surviving—*together.* I think you'll find that the hope you seize will be life itself.

4. Helping Your Children in the Aftermath

This chapter is written to any adult who has the responsibility for helping children through the grief and trauma of family suicide. The loss usually involves a parent or a brother or sister, though the suicide of a grandparent is becoming more commonplace each day. My aim is to offer solid, practical guidance, based on my experience and the best research on childhood grief following suicide. We are fortunate that several excellent studies have been carried out on just this subject.

Children have the same emotional needs after tragedy as adults, but their hurts are rarely taken seriously. Their friends don't usually come to see them. Their playmates can't afford to send flowers. They get some words of comfort and silent hugs from adults, but usually they are ignored by those who come to comfort the surviving adults. A recent study of thirty-six children who had lost parents by suicide showed that fully half of them were never even told the truth about the death of their parent! Some only learned the real story when they overheard adults discussing it or were able to read the death notice in the paper. When Howard Stone interviewed surviving spouses, he found that *none* of them knew how their children felt about the suicide of their other parent. The surviving parents had never asked their children about it! (Stone, *Suicide and Grief*, p. 52).

If you are a surviving spouse and a now-single parent, or if you have suffered the loss of one of your children through suicide, let me point out a potential problem at the beginning. Stone has noticed, and I agree, that the surviving parent who has trouble adapting to his or her own loss may also have trouble in raising the children. The blunt truth is that the children remain in *your* hands. Guiding them in the aftermath is *your* responsibility: you can't delegate it to someone else. It will be rough going to deal with your grief and theirs at the same time. But this investment in their future now will prevent more difficulty for all of you later. My prayer is that this chapter will help you to be sensitive to the needs of your children, and that, in the words of Rabbi Earl Grollman, "together, parent and child, you will try to build the temple of tomorrow's dreams upon the grave of yesterday's bitterness" (Grollman, *Talking About Death*, p. 67).

Explaining Suicide to Children

You will teach your children about suicide, whether you plan to or not. They will watch you and notice your responses. They will learn from you how they should act in the aftermath. So, decide *now* to be a good teacher. Act with the purpose of helping your children in the weeks and months ahead. Here are some essential guidelines for you to follow.

Be honest. You are sending constant messages to your children about this death in your family. Those messages need to be true. You need to explain clearly and directly what has happened, and why. Nothing but accurate information will do. This doesn't require explicit, gory details, but it does involve the simple truth. Use simple language that your children will understand, but make sure it's truthful language. Euphemisms such as "Your brother has gone to sleep" will only cause them to fear going to sleep themselves. They may never get over that fright. This fear of sleep is worsened whenever *you* prepare for bed. The children fear that they may lose you, too. Telling them "Daddy has gone on a long trip" will confuse them, and your lie will return to haunt you.

Avoid using God to explain the death. A little one's idea of a loving heavenly Father can be destroyed by the thoughtless "God wanted her more than we did" or "God sent an angel to take your daddy to heaven." All the child will hear is that her father is dead and that God is responsible for it. That is grim news for a child.

Honesty means telling the truth about suicide. Children want to know what suicide is, and why their family member did it. As Grollman emphasizes, "don't tell them what they'll need to unlearn later" (Grollman, *Talking About Death*, p. xiii). You can use the facts I have given in Chapter 1 to help your child get straight information. Be sure not to overexplain. Too much complicated information will only flood the child's mind and distract her from the reality of the death of her family member.

Listen carefully. Your children will have many questions to ask, and just as many strong feelings. Answer with the truth when you know it. When you don't know, don't be afraid to say so. You can expect *any* question to be raised. This is normal: *no question should be "unaskable" for your child.* You will hear questions like these: What did I do wrong? Was it my fault? Will I be punished? Was I bad or mean? Didn't he love me enough to want to live? Was he "crazy"? Where is Daddy now? Remember, nothing is off-limits. Let your children ask what's on their minds.

Listen between the lines as well. Children are skillful at asking two questions at once. "Do you still love me, Mommy?" may camouflage the child's *real* question: "Can I trust you not to leave me forever like Daddy did?"

Be careful about too much silence on your part. Children can misunderstand your long quiet periods. They might assume that you don't miss the deceased, that you don't care about the suicide, or that you're angry with them.

Be consistent. Don't confuse your child with two or three different versions of what happened. She will soon figure out that you can't be trusted for the truth, and she'll find someone else who can. You will have to repeat your explanations and assurances to your children. They will demand them from you, and they need them. So, stick to the simple truth and resist the temptation to soften or shade it.

Respect your child's senses and awareness. Real harm is done to communication between a parent and a child when the child sees all or part of the suicide but is told that the death was an accident. In one study, over one fourth of the children knew the most intimate details about the suicide. Yet they were told by their remaining parents that death had come from some natural cause. One girl saw her father's body hanging in the closet, yet her mother told her that he had died in a car wreck (Albert Cain and Irene Fast, "Children's Disturbed Reactions to Parent Suicide," in Cain, ed., *Survivors of Suicide,* p. 102). When such deception occurs, children begin to do one of two things. If they're small and easily manipulated, they begin to distrust their own senses. They wonder if anything they have heard or seen is real. If they're older, they see right through this charade and get angry at those who are lying to them. Trust will come hard for a young person who has been deceived and knows it.

Talk about the deceased family member. Focusing on the deceased will help the children realize that the death wasn't their fault, that they shouldn't blame themselves. And it helps combat a most serious problem afflicting suicide survivors: denial. Constant ventilation of their feelings about the deceased will remind the children that yes, their family member is dead, and yes, they can talk about it instead of keeping everything bottled up inside.

Rose Zeligs suggests that you avoid either blaming or praising the dead family member. Making him either a scapegoat or a hero will only confuse the children. Perhaps a more helpful practice would be to discuss better ways than suicide to handle problems, since your family member did not see any better way to solve his (Rose Zeligs, *Children's Experience with Death,* p. 173; Charles C Thomas, 1974).

Involve all your children. In the prominent study of thirty-six surviving children, the average age of those told nothing about the suicide was four years. Yet, as my four-year-old nephew reminds me, these very young children are curious, inquisitive, and aware of what is going on. They know that something terrible has happened. They can see who is weeping and who is no longer at home. Even though you'll have to gear your explanations to their level of understanding, they still deserve the truth. Overprotection and benevolent deception may backfire into distrust and resentment as the children grow up.

Don't go it alone. Your responsibility as a parent or guardian is tremendous. It can't be given away. However, at times it can be too much for you to bear by yourself. A pastor, counselor, or trusted friend can be a helpful cushion on which you can fall back when you need to. Such persons can serve as objective sounding boards for your grief, seeing things that you can't see and hearing things that you might better leave unsaid in front of the children. You might even want to try out your explanations on them first. They can offer you valuable emotional support for the task ahead. You need these "shock troops," for you have your own grieving to do as well.

HELPING YOUR CHILDREN GRIEVE

One of the destructive, silent myths about children and suicide holds that children do not grieve as deeply as adults. The myth states that children can be sad and hurt, but they never experience the anguish and gut-wrenching sorrow of profound grief. This myth is just that—a common belief with no basis in fact. The problem of grief is as staggering for children as it is for you, and they need your help here more than anywhere else.

Though their grief is felt as keenly as yours, children do not express their grief in the same ways that you do. They will act out their grief, both in their behavior and through physical symptoms. Yet they experience many of the same emotions that you do, some more deeply than you will. I want you to notice some emotional reactions for which you should be alert in your children. Then we'll examine the ways in which children and adolescents act out their feelings for us to see. One thing is important above all others. Your children *need* to grieve. Their emotions cry out for expression. Being upset is neither a crime nor a sin! You can help your children grieve by letting them see your tears, by crying with them, by letting them know it's O.K. to be upset. That's a gift that only you can give.

Guilt. Self-blame is quite common in surviving children, and it has many roots. Children often feel that they are responsible for the suicide, especially if an argument or angry scene happened shortly before the death. They will blame themselves for all manner of things, from being generally "bad" to costing too much. Also, if the child had a stormy relationship with the deceased before the suicide, it is likely that he at one time secretly wished the parent or sibling would die. This is common among children as well as adults. But when death does happen, the child is consumed with guilt. He is tormented by the question of whether the death was his fault. Small children are often caught up in the magical belief that their angry or jealous thoughts about the deceased directly caused the death. They will then take responsibility for the suicide upon themselves, yet remain silent about it. It usually goes unnoticed by surrounding adults.

Other roots of guilt abound. If the deceased had threatened or attempted suicide many times before the actual act, the child may have begun to feel exasperation about always having to live in the fear and tension of not knowing. The "I wish he'd do it and get it over with" feeling then becomes evident. Anger and contempt before suicide will turn into guilt after the death. When the child realizes the finality of this act, he will be overwhelmed with self-blame for being angry with the deceased.

Children also feel that they could have prevented the sui-

cide "if only." Stone points out that guilt is a major problem
for children who knew about the suicide's previous attempts
but conspired to keep them a secret. Many parents who
complete suicide tell their children in some way what is about
to happen. If the child knows and keeps that information to
himself, then guilt is certain to follow.

Psychiatrist Robert Jay Lifton coined the term "survivor
guilt" during his work with survivors of the atomic bomb
blasts at Hiroshima and Nagasaki. He believes that a child's
"survivor guilt" following suicide is a major factor in the
child's grief. When children are growing up, Lifton says, their
lives are full of little survivals. Every time Mommy and Daddy
leave, every spanking, every bedtime, every threat of rejection
(which Lifton calls a "death equivalent"), the child feels guilt
and blame. She asks herself, "What did I do to deserve that?"
But when a parent or sibling completes suicide, a child's
reservoir of guilt and blame suddenly overflows, posing a real
hazard to the child (Robert J. Lifton, *Death in Life*, quoted
in Klagsbrun, *Too Young to Die*, p. 106).

Klagsbrun tells of survivor guilt so intense that young people try to "atone" for it by their own act of suicide. Often they
complete suicide in order to be reunited in death with their
lost family member. As Klagsbrun accurately points out,
"children of suicides have a higher than average rate of suicide, not because the tendency toward suicide is biologically
inherited, but because they grow up with a heritage of guilt,
anger, and a sense of worthlessness" (Klagsbrun, *Too Young
to Die*, p. 106).

Klagsbrun tells of a college student who was four years old
when his father completed suicide. Listen as the young man
describes his own brand of "survivor guilt." In addition, no-

tice how deeply even four-year-olds experience the grief that follows suicide.

> I still suck my thumb, and I hate death. The thumb stands for my weakness, my inability to overcome it. I am afraid of death. . . . I was afraid, for years, to think of my father's death. I am afraid to think that the only relief from my guilt over his death can come from the ultimate psychological resolution of the desire to get back to him, to absolve myself in pure relation: to join him in death. I am afraid that what the Ouija board spelled out to me, that I would die when I was twenty-five, is true. I am afraid of my own power over myself, afraid of my father in me as death, afraid that guilt will seize my life. I hate death like I hate the father who won't let me use the force I need to not to be afraid. I am afraid of aggression, I am afraid of what will happen if I lose control. Somewhere in my head aggressive thoughts killed my father; the will came from the desire to have my mother all to myself. His death scared me from any such will in the future; I am afraid of my mother's implicit challenge to step forward and take his place. So I suck my thumb, am a nice boy, passive. I wouldn't hurt anyone. (In Klagsbrun, *Too Young to Die*, p. 107)

These severe reactions do not have to be. It depends in large part on your attitude and the care you give your children in the aftermath. This kind of intense guilt makes your child different from children who have lost family members in other ways. You should be prepared to deal with it.

How do you respond to such intense self-blame? Honest assurance and reassurance is necessary. Suicide is an act completed in solitude, and one person is responsible for it—*the deceased*. No person can make another person complete suicide. No person can singlehandedly prevent a suicide unless that person can live without sleep and spend twenty-four hours a day restraining the potential suicide. Your children aren't to blame; let them know you believe that.

Another necessary response is your own positive attitude toward your children. If your deceased family member had a bitter, hateful relationship with your son or daughter, it will be hard for you to avoid thoughts of blame toward this child. You alone can decide whether those thoughts are worth the loss of this child as well.

If it is obvious that the deceased, whether parent or child, died with unresolved anger at one of your children, you may need professional help to assist your own support of that child. Such obvious conflict will result in profound guilt for the child, and a good counselor should be brought in. Of course, this is and should always be an option for you in helping your children. When you can't do it alone, get help.

Denial and Disbelief. Once the immediate shock of *knowing* has occurred, children will often be tempted to escape from reality. They learn early how to play "pretend." This game soon escalates into "If I pretend this isn't happening, then it isn't." Parents often react with confusion when their children don't show any emotion at the death. Don't let this upset you. As Fady Hajal indicates in his excellent article, your children might "encapsulate" the memory of the deceased as though it belonged to them and no one else. In Hajal's study, one little girl showed no emotions following her father's suicide. Instead, she played house with her dolls. In her game, she kept "Daddy" as the central figure in her doll family, thus repressing the fact of his death. In this way she kept herself from shock and grief by pretending that nothing had happened (Hajal, "Post-Suicide Grief Work in Family Therapy," p. 38).

When denial breaks down, be prepared for the catch-up grieving that will need to take place as your child recovers what has earlier been denied. Gentle reassurance is again the best treatment.

Anger. I shall never forget the authentic rage expressed to me by a fourteen-year-old boy whose stepfather had completed suicide in their backyard. He had been the first person to the scene. When he saw what his stepfather had done, he angrily cursed the lifeless body. His grief continued to be expressed in the following weeks through alternating periods of sorrow and profound anger. In this case, anger was a necessary and normal first response for him. He had been subjected to much frustration and embarrassment by the stepfather, and his anger was justified. I encouraged him to get rid of it constructively, which he had already begun to do.

Anger will crop up in several forms among children. It may be directed toward the deceased for deserting the family and punishing all the family members with a last vengeful act. It may be aimed at the deceased's actions before the suicide as well. Anger may also be launched at *you,* for all sorts of real or imagined shortcomings in the situation. In fact, rage can lash out at anyone and everyone, from the coroner and the policeman to the funeral home, from smothering relatives to fawning clergy, from God himself to the world in general. What may appear as denial among your teen-age children may only be a rebellious, angry refusal to agree with *your* perception of what happened. A kind of blind rage will often be expressed by adolescents as they realize that they've been branded for all their world to see.

You'll need a thick skin and a long fuse to deal with this emotion. If anger is directed toward the deceased, resist the temptation to rush to his or her defense. Your child has every right to feel angry! Squashing this rage won't make it go away. Just as pressure cookers need ventilation to keep the powerful steam under control, so your children also share the same need. If the anger is directed toward you, be willing to absorb it without letting yourself be trampled. Communication is the key here: keep the channels open no matter what emotions may surface. Of course, if anger becomes violent and unmanageable, you'll need to seek professional help.

If anger is aimed toward another surviving child, you'll have to walk a tightrope to be fair to both sides. Of course, you won't be *objective;* you'll be a *parent.* That may mean stifling one child's anger in order to protect another's bruised self-esteem. Anger should not be allowed to degenerate into cruelty.

Fear. Suicide causes strong feelings of helplessness in children. Here this great tragedy has happened, and they were powerless to prevent it. Small children may begin to experience nightmares and bedwetting, and even a fear of going to sleep at night. Remember, such behavior is connected with their feelings. *What you're seeing is what is going on inside them.* If they start clinging to you, or refusing to be left with someone else, they're *afraid.* Situations that seem normal or only mildly upsetting to you will throw fearful children into a panic. Constant assurances of your love and presence are necessary. *Let them know that they have a future with you.*

Adolescents, like the college student quoted earlier, may fear that they've been "programmed" for suicide as they grow older. They need to know that suicide is an individual matter, that no matter how many family members do it, they can still choose *not* to. This explains why the "He was mentally ill" explanation can be destructive (unless "he" really was): your child may feel that he will inherit this mental illness and be compelled to suicide himself.

ACTING OUT CHILDHOOD GRIEF

Howard Stone has identified three ways in which your children may act out their grief after suicide (Stone, *Suicide and Grief*, pp. 52–53). The first involves complaints of *physical symptoms and illness*. Restlessness, constant nervous chatter, and increased energy often show up in grieving children. The surviving parents interviewed by Stone described a rash of illnesses in their children, ranging from minor colds and upset stomachs to influenza and more serious sickness. One child's latent diabetes appeared for the first time following the suicide of her father.

The second behavioral reaction is what I call the *"Man (or Woman) of the House" syndrome*, where the child attempts to take the place of the dead family member (usually the parent). I have often heard a grieving mother describe her adolescent son as "my little man" or "my rock of Gibraltar" in the days following the suicide of her husband. This tendency isn't necessarily harmful, but it leans dangerously in that direction. Listen to this father described by Stone, a man whose daughter began to assume the role of his deceased wife.

> She at the age of eleven or twelve assumed that she was just like my wife again. She was taking her [mother's] place in every way possible. She did her damnedest to cook meals, keep the house straightened up, even assuming some of the habits of her mother in cleaning the house, ways of doing the house, things that she'd never done before. . . . And she took over a wife's

role as much as a child could possibly do. . . . This went on
I'd say for just about a year pretty consistently. I finally realized
what was happening and that she was becoming so closely
attached to me that I realized I had to do something about it.
I started breaking away from her, doing more and more of
those things myself, which made it hard for me, too, but I
think in the long run it was the best thing. (Stone, *Suicide and
Grief*, pp. 52–53)

It was, indeed. Those well-meaning souls who bustle up to
your older children and exclaim, "Now, you've got to be brave
and take care of your dear mother (or father)," do your children great harm. You have to ensure that this doesn't happen.
Don't make your children take care of you. A fourteen- or
fifteen-year-old boy is not prepared to be either the "man of
the house" or your substitute husband. Also, be careful about
forcing your surviving children to make up for the loss of a
child who completes suicide. No one can replace a lost family
member—no one. And no one should ever be the square peg
forced into a round hole.

The third kind of acting out mentioned by Stone may
already be obvious to you. Children occasionally become
problem children or delinquents who demonstrate their anger
to the world by rebelling against everything. Their grades
drop at school, their attitude deteriorates at home, and the
older ones often just pack up and leave. Be prepared for this
by alerting principals, teachers, and guidance counselors to
the special needs of your children. If your church employs a
minister to youth, or has someone especially trained in working with young people, that person should be informed about
your child's needs. Other adults like these who treat your
child with dignity and respect can often break the ice and

establish a friendship on which a young person can lean when things get rough.

You can't guarantee good results from the grief process through which your children are going. You can only do your best with the help of God and those you love. If everything tumbles in, don't let yourself go with it. There are limits to what you can do, and the bottom line is your own sanity. Remember, you can't help anyone if you're falling apart. Do what you can do, get help for what you can't do, and trust God for the process.

AFTERCARE OF YOUR CHILDREN

Your family won't always be in turmoil, though that promise may ring hollow now. Things *will* get better. Your children *will* recover, in time. Here are some things to tie a string around for future reference, when the shock and trauma are easing.

1. Watch anniversaries, birthdays, and special holidays. These days will be rough on all of you. Yet your family traditions need to be maintained, in spite of the pain. These special times can provide strength to your family and give you a chance to grow closer together. Father's Day and Mother's Day will be especially difficult if a parent died. Christmas will be the most painful of all, especially the first one after the suicide. Two of the most agonizing times for the children will be the birthday of the deceased and the anniversary of the suicide. I urge you to continue to observe both of these. Don't pretend that those days are ordinary now; neither of them will ever be "just another day" for you or your children. These days can provide you times to remember the deceased in your

own way, and to make a part of your lives those things about him that you treasure. If they do nothing else, these days remind you, twice a year, that you were hit with a terrible tragedy and still *survived! That* you ought never to take for granted.

2. Special event father-son and mother-daughter activities are often standard in churches and schools during the adolescent years. If a parent has been lost through suicide, the pain of being different will be even greater for the surviving children at these times. Give them a chance to choose other adults to escort them to these occasions, perhaps close relatives or family friends. The fact of suicide will always be there for them, and the world will not help them cope with it. They must cope with it on their own initiative, when they are ready. It is no disrespect to the deceased for your children to adjust their lives in this way toward more joy and happiness. Such adjustment is to be encouraged and applauded.

3. When your children reach adolescence and experience the normal teen-age crises of self-esteem, they will have a convenient, ready-made crutch: "The others don't like me because my father (mother) killed himself (herself)." Encourage them to leave that kind of attitude behind them as they mature. It probably isn't true to begin with, and it isn't fair to all the other teen-agers out there jostling for attention with their own handicaps. Your children have a right to be liked or disliked for the same reasons as everyone else, and their friends have a right to like or dislike them for such reasons.

4. Teach your children to be selective about who they tell the story of the suicide. They are under no moral compulsion to volunteer this information to future insurance agents and thus pay ridiculous rates the rest of their lives. Let them be

judicious about this knowledge, and they may retain some control over how much future hurt they will have to bear.

5. Grandparents are usually involved in the suicide grief of a family. They need to be! They have much to offer your children. If your spouse completed suicide, his parents will also be desperately grieved. One of their links to him will be your children. They didn't stop being grandparents when your family member died. And your children will need to continue cultivating those relationships with their grandparents. Here is a potential resource for you, depending, of course, on your relationship with your in-laws and with your own parents.

In his book *God Bless You, Mr. Rosewater,* Kurt Vonnegut, Jr., wrote: "Sons of suicides seldom do well" (quoted in Klagsbrun, *Too Young to Die,* p. 106). We hear in that brief line all the pain and damage that we see in the lives of surviving children. Yet this does not have to be the last word. Your sons and daughters can freely choose how well they will "do." One of my dearest friends is the son of a suicide. He is a paragon of personal integrity, of "togetherness." He has "done well," to be sure. And he has helped me toward the success that he has found in his life of responsibility before God. So, you see, it's up to each one of you! Lives are being changed for the better as you read this, perhaps *because* you're reading this. Your sensitivity to the needs of your children may well be the shining light in the darkness of despair that helps them find their way back home. I hope this brief chapter will minister to you in that journey.

5. Suicide and Your Faith

Suicide can throw your religious life for a loop. It temporarily destroys your reservoir of good feelings about yourself, about God, and about life in general. It disrupts your religious "rhythm." In this chapter, I want to share some facts and feelings about your faith and future in the aftermath of suicide. I hope we can puncture a few of the blown-up religious myths about suicide, and help you recover the rhythm of your faith.

I am writing as a Christian minister. I assume that most of those reading this book will be either Christian or Jewish, or of some other religious faith that has been shaped by these two traditions. Even if you have no professed religious belief, this chapter should be helpful because it discusses the past and present laws relating to suicide, most of which have been based upon the Jewish and Christian traditions.

People are going to bombard you with "facts" about "what the Bible says" about suicide. Have the facts straight for yourself. No two authors on the subject can agree on how many times the Bible refers to suicide, since everyone uses a different working definition. I will set out in this chapter every major Jewish and Christian tradition about suicide.

Most of these accounts deal with self-inflicted death. Others come close to what has been called "assisted suicide"—i.e., the person has himself killed by someone else. Still others involve group death, where one does and takes others with him or where entire groups complete mass suicide. All these stories shed light on how other religious persons have understood this age-old problem. After you finish this chapter, you will be able to know for yourself what the Bible says and what it doesn't say about suicide.

We will also look at Christian church history. You will see the foundations for later laws and prohibitions against suicide, as well as for the stigmas that attached themselves to the act. This section is heavily weighted by the Catholic tradition, for the simple reason that Protestants have largely ignored this issue until this century.

After the brief survey is completed, I offer two additional bits of help. The first is a way to confront the tragedy of suicide and still "think straight" about God. The second involves some suggestions as to how you can regain the rhythm of your religious life, and even improve it, in the aftermath.

SUICIDE IN JEWISH TRADITION

Despair and anguish are as common in the Hebrew scriptures as are joy and celebration. Death hurt as much then as it does now. We should not be surprised at the many characters in the Jewish story who chose to escape from the burdens of life through the act of suicide. And for every person who completed the act, many more wished to die and be rescued from their distressing existence.

Moses, Elijah, and Jonah of the Hebrew Bible, Tobit and
Sarah of the Book of Tobit—all prayed at one time that God
would take their lives and end their misery. The writer of
Ecclesiastes spoke in despair of an existence where the dead
are more fortunate than the living, where "better . . . is he
who has not yet been, and has not seen the evil deeds that
are done under the sun" (Eccles. 4:3). Jeremiah lamented,
and Job cursed, the day he was born. Yet none of these people
were singled out by the Old Testament and intertestamental
writers for condemnation. The Hebrew writers understood
depression and despair. Suicide is merely *reported* in their
scriptures: no approval or disapproval is given. Only in the
Talmud is the act specifically condemned, and it was not
written and codified until the Christian era. Modern Jewish
scholars believe that the harshest Jewish treatment of suicides
was due partly to the influence of the negative Christian
environment on the subject (Ch. W. Reines, "The Jewish
Attitude Toward Suicide," *Judaism*, Vol. 10, Spring 1961, p.
170).

Look briefly at these accounts in Hebrew history of the act
of suicide. This will give you at least a partial glimpse of what
the Bible says. The Old Testament accounts include the
stories of Abimelech (Judg. 9:50–55), Samson (Judg. 16:
23–31), Saul (I Sam. 31:1–6; II Sam. 1:1–27; I Chron. 10:
1–14), Ahithophel (II Sam. 17:23), and Zimri (I Kings
16:8–20). Abimelech had his armor bearer kill him in order
to avoid the "disgrace" of dying at the hand of a woman.
Ahithophel hanged himself. Zimri burned a building down
upon himself. Samson pulled a building full of Philistines
down upon himself, praying to God that he might die as well.
Saul's death is recorded in three separate and contradictory

accounts. We must assume that he either ran himself through with his sword or had a bystander do it for him.

Most of these people were given honorable burials. No moral comment is ever given about the manner of their deaths. In fact, Saul is treated as a great servant of God (II Samuel) and Samson is later hailed in the New Testament as one of the great heroes of faith "of whom the world was not worthy" (Heb. 11:38).

Two accounts exist from the Maccabean period. *Razis,* an elder of Jerusalem during the Maccabean revolt, killed himself to avoid being taken captive by the Syrian general Nicanor (II Macc. 14:37–46). The mother of seven sons murdered by Antiochus IV threw herself upon their funeral pyre (IV Macc. 17:1f).

In the first century A.D., two accounts were recorded by Jewish historians. The first involved a group of Jewish soldiers under the command of the young priest Josephus. After being surrounded by Roman soldiers for 47 days, the group entered into a pact of assisted suicide. Each man killed his neighbor, except for Josephus, who surrendered to the Roman general. Six years later, in A.D. 73, a group of 953 Jews on the rock fortress of Masada completed mass suicide to avoid capture by the advancing Romans.

The Talmud, or repository of Jewish oral tradition, considered many stories of suicide and condemned it in most of them. On the basis of their interpretation of Gen. 9:5—"For your lifeblood I will surely require a reckoning"—the rabbis considered suicide a grave sin. The only exceptions to the formal condemnations were those situations where a Jew was forced to betray his faith under torture, commit another grave sin (such as adultery), or endanger his country in wartime.

These condemnations were rarely carried out in practice. The Jews did not consider a self-inflicted death to be suicide unless it was announced beforehand and then carried out in front of eyewitnesses. Even a person found hanging was given the benefit of the doubt—it could have been an accident! Minors and mentally ill persons were exempt from condemnation, no matter what the situation. If a person killed himself to make restitution for past sins, even that was acceptable to the community.

No recrimination toward either the victim or his family occurs in modern Judaism. Although the act of suicide itself still meets with condemnation, on the conviction that life is always worth living, the Jewish community recognizes the unique situation of the victim and the family and tries to treat everyone involved with sensitivity and consideration. A realistic flexibility is employed, along with an appreciation for the best psychiatric information available.

SUICIDE IN CHRISTIAN TRADITION

The only recorded suicide in the New Testament is that of Judas Iscariot, and only one of three Christian traditions records it as such. In Matthew's account (Matt. 27:5), Judas kills himself by hanging. In Luke's account (Acts 1:16–20), he mysteriously falls down and bursts open. A third tradition, that of Papias, bishop of Hierapolis, comes a hundred years after the fact. As recorded by Eusebius, Papias tells us that Judas swelled up and was crushed in a narrow street by a wagon. However we reconcile these differing traditions about Judas' death, we must remember this: nowhere is suicide ever mentioned as the reason for his condemnation by the church.

The New Testament and the early church both regarded Judas as a traitor and a "devil" *because he betrayed Jesus,* and only for that reason. I believe that if we accept the account that Judas *did* complete suicide, then we have clear evidence that he repented of his betrayal and presumably completed suicide as an act of restitution. He certainly can bear no greater burden of guilt with regard to his betrayal than can Simon Peter, who three times denied knowing Jesus.

Suicide became a serious problem for the early church. Under great persecution for their beliefs, thousands of believers desired to die and go to be with their risen Lord. We even hear echoes of this sentiment in the letters of Paul: "For me . . . to die is gain. . . . My desire is to depart and be with Christ, for that is far better" (Phil. 1:21, 23).

Ignatius, bishop of Antioch, gives us a classic example of how suicidal desires for martyrdom reached a fever pitch in the early church. In his letter to the Romans, he prayed that the wild beasts might devour him and thus let him reach the presence of Jesus Christ. "Let all come, fire and cross and conflicts with beasts, hacking, cutting, wrenching of bones, chopping of limbs, the crushing of my body, cruel chastisement of the devil laid upon me. Only let me attain to Jesus Christ" (Ignatius, *To the Romans* 5.3, in *The Early Christian Fathers,* ed. and tr. by Henry Bettenson, p. 46; Oxford University Press, 1969).

The early church was also marked by a few ecstatic groups of believers who completed mass suicide in much the same attitude as Ignatius shows above. The early church fathers, while disapproving of this mass rush to death, did approve of suicide in order to avoid rape or forced denial of one's faith.

Augustine and Thomas Aquinas stand out as the main

shapers of Catholic thought on the subject of suicide. Both spoke forcefully against it, and both were instrumental in leading the church to adopt strict prohibitions and recriminations against the act. They considered it to be a form of murder, and thus a mortal sin. It ruled out any opportunity for repentance. It was further an attack upon society and upon the sovereignty of God. Protestants have been heavily influenced by these teaching, and may quite firmly believe them also.

Modern Catholic theology distinguishes between "direct" and "indirect" suicide. Direct suicide is desired self-murder and is always a mortal sin. Indirect suicide results when death is not desired but rather allowed that a greater good might occur. For example, the soldier who falls on a live grenade to save his comrades completes "indirect" suicide, which is considered both lawful and worthy of praise by the church.

The Roman Catholic canon law still prescribes severe penalties for suicides and attempted suicides. This probably accounts for the more severe guilt problems that Catholic survivors experience. In actual practice, though, the Catholic Church seldom makes judgments on those who take their own lives. Realizing the tremendous mental anguish and trauma at work within the suicidal situation, the church usually allows full burial rites for the victim. The church realizes now that its main focus must be a caring ministry to the survivors rather than punishments against the deceased and his family.

Protestant thought on suicide is sketchy at best, but it reveals a history just as harsh as that of the earlier Roman Church. No less a leader than John Wesley advocated the public hanging of the bodies of victims and the dragging of the naked bodies of female victims through the streets. Modern Protestant scholars, most notably Karl Barth, Dietrich Bonhoeffer, and Helmut Thielicke, came to a more humane understanding of the problem. All three spoke of the sinful nature of the act, but they also stressed the forgiveness of God for all sins, even the act of suicide. This has been the approach of most modern Protestant groups. Their primary focus is in ministering to suicide survivors, though the quality of this ministry certainly varies among congregations.

THINKING STRAIGHT ABOUT GOD

You have seen what the Judeo-Christian traditions have said about suicide. You have also seen in this book some of the brutalities that have been carried out against suicides and their families in the name of the Almighty. No wonder so many fists are shaken at organized religion over this issue! When more humane and merciful treatment began to be extended to suicides and their families, religious people were all too often at the tail end of the line.

Things *are* different now. Times, people, and theologies are changing. The church is eager to help you think straight about God in the aftermath of your tragedy. We can begin this task by focusing on some of the religious questions for which you are seeking answers.

Is suicide the "unpardonable sin"? Traditional Roman Catholic theology has held suicide to be a mortal sin, partly because it is believed to preclude any possibility for repentance. Protestant theology has offered a necessary correction to this view. As both Barth and Bonhoeffer pointed out, *many* people die suddenly without having "repented" of all their

sins. To make the last millisecond of a person's life so su-
premely important is to misunderstand both the worth of our
lives and the forgiveness of God. Our lives aren't games of
high-stakes poker, where one final hand can wipe you out.
God judges our lives in their totality. If we accept the premise
that God's nature is one of steadfast love and mercy, then we
must say with Barth: "If there is forgiveness of sins at all,
. . . there is surely forgiveness for suicide" (Karl Barth, *Church
Dogmatics*, Vol. III/4, p. 405; tr. by A. T. Mackay et al.; T.
& T. Clark, 1961).

You need to rid yourself of the superstition that all suicides
go to hell. This often results from a rigid logic which teaches
that forgiveness occurs only *after* repentance. I believe the
wealth of the Biblical evidence shows that God's grace and
mercy are unmerited, given freely. We don't *earn* his love, we
receive it! We're able to repent and change our lives *because
we have been forgiven*. That's the good news I want you to
hear. Your family member exists in the mercy and forgiveness
of God. Already, in the midst of this tragedy, God is working
to create goodness out of the ashes of your despair.

Why did God do this to me? It's not unnatural for you to
feel like shaking your fist at God. The first thing most of us
do when we're hurting is find someone or something to blame
for our pain. Yet I caution you against using God as your
scapegoat. He can handle it, but I'm not sure you can. When
the acute grief is over, you and God will still be around. I
would hate to see your relationship fall apart over the tragedy
of suicide.

God has created us as free persons, not puppets or robots.
We can freely choose the paths our lives will take. We can
even choose to die, if we wish. God doesn't have everything

in our lives planned out in advance. That kind of determinism makes us little more than wind-up dolls or computers programmed for specific functions.

In other words, God didn't "take" your family member. God didn't "need" your husband, wife, or child more than you did, as some will piously say to you. Suicide is a human act, done for human reasons, attempted and completed by human beings. That fact hurts us, because it tells us we've been rejected and deserted by someone we love. But it's the truth, plain and simple. Those who tell you that all this is happening to you in order to make you "a stronger person" or "a better Christian" offer you cold comfort. Again, they present God as the player and we persons as mere pawns on the chessboard.

Our lives are not obedience schools where we are whipped and cajoled into line against our will. If we believe in free will, we realize that God has created us as free persons. We can and do make wrong choices and destructive decisions. When we foul our water and air, we don't blame the pollution on God. We flatten cities with strategic bombings and take full credit for it. We can even take our own lives if we want to, and no one can stop us, because we're free. That means we can't cry "The devil made me do it" or "It must be God's will" when we make destructive choices. Unless you are psychotic, *you* are responsible for your actions, and you alone. Pulling in "the devil" or God is a convenient cop-out, and it can be destructive to your religious life.

Where is God, then, in this tragedy? I remember two stories that speak to this question of where God is in your situation. Both deal with wartime events. The first is found in *Night,* a book by Elie Wiesel, a survivor of Auschwitz, the infamous German concentration camp.

> The SS hanged two Jewish men and a youth in front of the whole camp. The men died quickly, but the death throes of the youth lasted for half an hour. "Where is God? Where is he?" someone asked behind me. As the youth still hung in torment in the noose after a long time, I heard the man call again, "Where is God now?" And I heard a voice in myself answer, "Where is he? He is here. He is hanging there on the gallows . ." (Elie Wiesel, *Night,* p. 75; quoted in Jürgen Moltmann, *The Crucified God,* pp. 273–274; tr. by R. A. Wilson and John Bowden; Harper & Row, 1974)

The second story involves a pastor called hurriedly to the family of a young soldier killed in Vietnam. The mother was speechless with grief, but the father was livid with anger. Pacing the floor, he shouted at the minister: "Preacher, I just want you to answer me one thing. Where was God when my boy stepped on that mine? Where was your God when my boy died?" The minister lowered his head and replied in a sad, distant voice: "Where was he? The same place he was when *his* Son died."

For years, the Christian churches held to the dogma that God didn't "feel" things, that he didn't suffer. In the light of the torment of Auschwitz, the horror of Hiroshima, the agony of Vietnam, the tragedy of suicide, we recognize such theology today to be morally bankrupt. As Jürgen Moltmann says so forcefully: "There cannot be any other Christian answer to the question of this torment. To speak here of a God who could not suffer would make God a demon. To speak here of an absolute God would make God an annihilating nothingness. To speak here of an indifferent God would cor

demn men to indifference" (Moltmann, *The Crucified God,*
p. 274). The cross remains our testimony to "where God is"
in our deepest tragedies. He hangs there before us, bearing
our pain, feeling our hurts, conquering our death.

An answer that makes some sense. When we face suicide,
we confront a mystery. No one knows just what goes on in
the mind and heart of a person before suicide. What we
perceive as self-murder may be an act of loving self-sacrifice.
The starting point for any serious religious statement about
suicide must be the confession of *mystery.* Suicide is an act
of solitude. We can't always form a judgment, and we should
not, about why a person chooses death in this manner.

I find the proposal of Robert Neale to be helpful as one way
of making some faith-ful sense of this tragedy. Neale points
out that traditional theology has always seen suicide as an
attack on God, a rebellious attempt to seize his power for
human purposes. But this point of view causes problems for
our view of death. In this conception, Neale says, "Godly"
death can only come *from without.* Only war, accident, or
disease become legitimate ways to die, apart from natural
causes. Anyone who attempts or completes suicide is then refusing the divine gift of life. Neale seriously questions this view.

> The suicide may not want to destroy the life given by God; he
> may want to destroy the life given by Satan, the life given over
> to the power of sin. He desires to destroy the life which leads
> to death. It is the life given by God which he has lost and hopes
> to regain. The suicide is a sinner who attacks God, but he may
> also be a child of God who is attacking the god of theologians.
> (Robert E. Neale, *The Art of Dying,* p. 65; Harper & Row,
> 1973)

Neale shows us one way that faithful Christians can view
the act of suicide. What is needed in our ministry is not more
condemnation, more law, more stigmatizing. We cannot
praise those who matter-of-factly rule out eternal life for the
suicide as if that matter had been decided beforehand. The
Bible certainly refuses that approach. We are not in the
business of passing judgment on those who can no longer
defend themselves. As Presbyterian pastor, John Sutherland
Bonnell, wrote twenty years ago: "At best we may leave this
issue in the hands of a God who is perfectly just as well as
loving and merciful" (John Sutherland Bonnell, "The Ultimate in Escape," *Pastoral Psychology*, Vol. 9, Feb. 1958, pp.
20–28).

Your Religious Life in the Aftermath

Suicide is a religious issue in its own right. As we have seen,
it is bound to affect your religious life. You may even turn
away from your church for a while. This absence can be a
helpful time of "fasting" after the forced worship of the
funeral and graveside services. Or you may throw yourself into
your church's work, doing all things to avoid the fear of doing
nothing. Whatever your own response, your experience of
this crisis will be felt in your religious life. I want to share
these guidelines, or suggestions, or "props," to help you in
rediscovering "the joy of your salvation."

Allow God into your situation. Let God help you in your
weakness, in *this* situation. Shed the camouflage of denial
with him. If you're overcome by weakness, remember the
promise of Paul: "The Spirit helps us in our weakness; for we
do not know how to pray as we ought, but the Spirit himself

intercedes for us with sighs too deep for words" (Rom. 8:26).

Allow your church to care for you. Learn to recognize their loving concern in whatever shape it appears. When they come to care, let them into your life. You need it, you deserve it, and God wants you to have that fellowship. True "charity" is no shame; it is the perfection of Christian love.

Ask your theological questions when you're ready. Don't be afraid to question God—the greatest religious figures in history have done so. Don't be afraid to ask *anything*—God can handle your questions. Find yourself a helpful, sensitive pastoral counselor who can help you form your questions and seek for answers. Remember, your answers must be *yours.* If these answers don't make sense in your situation, find some that do. You don't have to accept my word or anyone else's about *where* God is or *why* this happened. But you do need some help in the asking.

Express your emotions faith-fully. If you're mad at God, tell *him.* Whatever you tell God is a form of prayer. If you need forgiveness, ask for it. Jesus made that an essential part of his model prayer, and we would do well to follow that pattern.

Take advantage of opportunities for worship. True worship can't be done alone for long. It can't be "seen" on the television screen or "heard" on the radio. Christ showed great wisdom when he promised his presence *wherever two or three* are gathered together. It's the gathering that makes all the difference.

Practice the presence of God daily. "Go into your room," as Jesus advised, sometime each day. There may be times when you want to go in there and scream in God's presence. At other times there will be outpourings of grief, which I call "spasms of the soul." Take time daily to invite God into your life, no matter what you're feeling. Pray. Read the "great pages" from Scripture. Let God give you his gifts as he will.

Allow closure to come to your grief—in God's presence. Just as it is necessary that you grieve over your loss, it will also be necessary for you to close the wound in your life and allow it to heal over. There will be a scar. It will always be sensitive to the touch, but the current stabbing pain will gradually subside and then disappear. I have included at the end of this book a memorial service to be observed one year following the suicide. It can be held in your church, your home, or perhaps in a cherished spot where your family shared good times together. The service marks the end of the period of "postvention" after your loss. It calls you before God to the challenge of letting go and building a new life for the future.

I suggest that you gather your family and friends together for this service, with the leadership of your pastor. Let this be the occasion for new beginnings in your life—a chance, not to worship the past and its memories, but rather to build upon them for *your* future. This is a way of thanking God for bringing you through the struggle. It's an opportunity to commit to him now, for his watchful care and love, the life *and* death of your family member.

6. Living as a Suicide Survivor

The title of this final chapter goes out on a limb. It assumes that you do want to continue living throughout the aftermath of suicide. If this assumption is correct, then the issues with which I deal in this chapter are *your* issues. They will not all apply to you directly, but they should each prove to be valuable. I am delighted with your decision to be a *survivor*. Now let's look at some problems of living that you will face "out there."

DEALING WITH THE SLURS ABOUT SUICIDE

Stigma is one of our most expressive words. It came to us from the Greeks, who used it to refer to the branding mark placed on a slave by his or her master. The apostle Paul uses this word in a similar fashion in his letter to the Galatians, speaking of the wounds and scars he received in his Christian missionary activity. "From now on let no one cause trouble for me, for I bear on my body the brand marks *(stigmata)* of Jesus" (Gal. 6:17).

When we speak of a stigma today, we usually refer to a wound of a different kind: the disgrace and reproach expressed by others. The force, the impact of such a social stigma is branded just as deeply into your life as if it were carved there with a knife or seared with a hot iron. Erich Lindemann, a pioneer in the study of acute grief, tells of a man whose father had completed suicide many years before. Reaching back to his memories of the Old Testament to describe his feelings of being stigmatized, the man referred to his father's suicide as the time when "he placed the mark of Cain upon me" (Erich Lindemann and Ina May Greer, "A Study of Grief: Emotional Responses to Suicide," in Cain, ed., *Survivors of Suicide*, p. 67). That image of being branded probably describes pretty accurately how you feel. Like Abel's brother Cain, you've been marked with an emotional imprint that you'll carry with you the rest of your life (Gen. 4:15). Cain's mark, however, was for his *protection*. What are you going to do with yours? Will it mean a mark of doom or a signal of survival? Only you can decide how you will let the stigma of suicide affect your life.

Less than a century ago the stigma of suicide didn't have to be imagined by the survivors: it was malignantly real. Bodies of suicides were not only denied burial in consecrated ground, they were required to be buried by night, at a crossroads, with stakes driven through their hearts. The hands and head were often cut off and buried apart from the body. Families had to forfeit to the state all property owned by the victim, for suicide was considered treason against the king. Trials were held over the corpse. The body was "sentenced" to be beaten with chains and burned. Members of the suicide's family frequently had to pay the victim's in-laws for the shame that the suicide had brought to them.

Things are radically different today. Few official taboos remain against suicide or against your family. The state doesn't punish you for what your family member has done. Most of the punishment you will receive, if any, will come from your "friends" and your own family.

Suicide survivors consistently report more feelings of stigma and shame than do those experiencing normal grief. However, much of this may be more imagined than real. You will experience some blame, to be sure. Some will be subtle, and some quite blunt, but it will come your way. But don't start seeing an "enemy" behind every rock. Not everyone will feel what you tend to assume they feel. If you start breaking ties with close friends and co-workers over what you think they're thinking, you may well be left on your island of isolation with no one to help you find rescue.

I agree with those who believe in openness and honesty on your part. Most suicide survivors aren't very honest with their close friends about the nature of the death. This only hurts you, because you are always left to wonder if and how much they "know." Such a constant state of not knowing doesn't *help* you work through your grief. It *hinders* you. It leads toward inevitable isolation and loneliness. One man found much anxiety in his refusal to tell the truth about the suicide of his wife, who was dying of cancer.

A neighbor bugged me about that. And she doesn't know, I didn't tell her. Her house is from here to the door from our house, and to see my wife get in a cab in the driveway, the neighbor says can I help you and she says, no, thank you very much for everything . . . so probably that stirred her curiosity. When people asked me how she died, in the hospital, I say yeah, in the hospital, or something like that. I felt funny about telling a lie, and yet I wanted to skirt this deal. (In Stone, *Suicide and Grief*, pp. 86–87)

Members of a suicide's family often tend to see the death as a family disgrace, a skeleton to be hidden from view in the closet. They talk of "dishonor," "a blot on our good name," and frequently resort to denial to avoid this perceived shame. The spouse, however, is singled out for the greatest blame. As Phyllis Silverman points out, "The suicide leaves his wife (or her husband) a legacy that keeps her married to him (or him married to her) *because of this guilt by association*" (Phyllis Rolfe Silverman, "Intervention with the Widow of a Suicide," in Cain, ed., *Survivors of Suicide*, p. 210). Women may feel some stigma because they are "without a man" in a male-dominated society. Suicide spouses feel immediately the difference between other widowed spouses and themselves. This often prevents them from getting involved in support groups for widowed spouses. It also poses problems for meeting new friends and for future dating, since "telling" presents some risks to new relationships.

You may be unfortunate enough to live in what Albert Cain and Irene Fast call a "blaming community" (Cain and Fast, "The Legacy of Suicide: Observations on the Pathogenic Impact of Suicide upon Marital Partners,"in Cain, ed., *Survivors of Suicide*, p. 148). Schoolmates taunt your children, neighbors heap blame upon you, and your family and in-laws aim their fingers at you. You hear statements like "I'm not surprised it happened" and "She drove him to it." These people dissect your marriage in public. Their goal is to "draw blood" from you and your children through their malicious gossip. In this extreme kind of situation, which rarely happens, suicide survivors find literally no support for their shattered lives. Their feelings of shame go sky-high. Their grief gets hopelessly stuck because they can't talk about it to anyone. So they retreat into their homes, or change their phone numbers, or eventually move away. If you find yourself in this kind of situation, I see no point in continuing to be the bull's-eye for their target practice. Moving away is no disgrace when you do it for the right reasons. In this case, your move isn't made out of denial, but rather as protection for you and your family. Remember, you and your children are your first priority.

Finding a New Place Where You Are

I've written a lot already about the importance of being open and honest with yourself during this crisis. Honesty with others is just as crucial, as we have seen. You are now the survivor of a suicide. That will be but one of your identities in the years ahead. Now, you don't have to put that fact in the Yellow Pages or on your rear bumper in order to be honest with it. You only have to accept it as *part* of who you are. One way of doing that is to adopt a practice of openness with others with regard to the suicide.

Listen to these words from a suicide widow who decided *not* to hide the truth.

> I'd tell anybody that asks me. You know, when they hear I'm a widow they say, oh, did your husband have an accident and I say no, he committed suicide. If I lied to them I'd be lying to myself. . . . It's lying because if I said yes, he had an accident, and then they got to know you later and they heard that he

committed suicide, they want to know gee, I wonder why she's
hiding it, you know. (In Stone, *Suicide and Grief*, p. 87)

This woman has made the crucial decision that I hope you'll
make. In accepting the label "suicide survivor," she has decided to focus, not on suicide, but on *survival*. She wants to
live! She affirms the fact, without any attempt to hide it, that
she has come through her own public hell and *survived*.
That's the first step toward finding a new place where you are.
In your continuing course on suicide grief, I hope you'll major
in survival.

You can make a new place for yourself. You can change
your corner of the world for the better. Let's look at some
ways to accomplish this renovation.

You'll have to develop your own timetable for coming out
of your extended grief. When you're ready, and only when
you are ready, you can start exchanging your old "place" for
a new one where you are. Some suicide survivors will wear
black clothes and long veils for the rest of their lives. They're
stuck, frozen in acute grief. I hope you'll choose life.

You may want to "make yourself over" with some new
clothes or a fashionable hairstyle. These things give a sense
of newness to many people. Think about learning to do the
something you've always wanted to do. Go back to school and
finish your degree, or get involved in some community project. Go to your pastor and volunteer for one of those church
jobs for which no one ever volunteers. As a pastor, I can tell
you how glad your minister will be to see you! But I want to
caution you to wait until you're ready for all this. Don't use
a sudden, frantic "flight into activity" as a way of avoiding
your grief. When your grief is running its course and begin-

ning to subside, then take the opportunities before you. You owe it to yourself and to your family.

FINDING A COMPANY OF UNDERSTANDING PEOPLE

During the early stages of your suicide grief, you probably felt a strong need to just be left alone. The strain of funeral arrangements, having to play host or hostess to other mourners, and your own sense of "fallingapartness" drives you frequently to seek silence and solitude. As one suicide widow said so clearly:

> I did not want anybody—it's like a wounded animal, you want to go away and lick your wounds and heal. You want to lie down and bleed to death, but do it by yourself, and when you're ready to get up, you get up. . . . They kept saying, you have to have people with you. I said no . . . I've got to face these ghosts. I've got to live in this house. Let me work it out. (In Stone, *Suicide and Grief,* p. 30)

As the worst part of your bereavement begins to recede, you *can* be strengthened and uplifted by a caring group of friends who understand. These "support groups" can be found in a number of places. Many churches have groups for people going through grief. These usually run continually, with members entering and leaving on their own timetables. If your church doesn't have such a group, you might suggest to your pastor that one be formed.

Community mental health centers offer therapy groups into which you may want to look. Also, investigate the local chapter of organizations such as Parents Without Partners and Widowed Persons' Service. If you lost your child through suicide, get in touch with a local chapter of The Compassion-

ate Friends, a self-help group for parents whose children have
died. There are more than two hundred chapters in the
United States. You can receive information about one close
to you by writing: The Compassionate Friends; P.O. Box
1347; Oak Brook, Illinois 60521. Still another option would
be for you to organize such a group yourself. The Compassionate Friends was started by Arnold and Paula Shamres
after their ten-year-old daughter was killed in an accident.
Since then, their efforts have meant the difference to thousands of bereaved parents.

Don't be afraid to ask for help from those close to you when
you need it. So much hurt and pain go unheeded during grief
because we don't want to bother anyone else with our problems. Wouldn't you want someone close to you to ask for help
if they needed it? They probably stand ready to aid you if
you'll tell them how they can help and just where it hurts.

Finding a Good Counselor

I am a strong supporter of competent counseling. My experience as a pastor, youth minister, and chaplain proved to me
that competent counseling really makes a difference in people's lives. Thank God that the stigma of seeing someone for
professional help is slowly but surely diminishing in our country. A whole new generation of trained pastoral counselors is
out on the front line of human crises, working to bring about
healing in the lives of the people they touch. Communities
are awake to the need for mental health services. Psychiatrists
are finally being recognized for the valuable work they do,
instead of being made the butt of uninformed "shrink" jokes.

You shouldn't have to search too hard for a kind, competent counselor. Start with your pastor, especially if he or she has professional training. Your minister will have the best knowledge of your situation. It is hoped that he or she will have been working with you in "postvention" since the day of the suicide. Your pastor's counseling ministry is provided by the congregation. This help should therefore not burden you financially. At this place in your recovery, that in itself will be important to you. Other ministers are also possibilities for you. Your pastor may not feel comfortable in such a counseling situation, or you may feel that it would be helpful to you to tell your story to a stranger.

If the pastoral avenue is closed to you, consult with your family doctor or your local mental health agency. You will be referred to several persons from whom you can choose one to visit. Ask about fees and payments at the beginning. Check also to see if your health insurance will cover the charges. Many counselors operate on a sliding fee-scale depending on your ability to pay.

Be sure to take care of yourself in this area. Only then can you be of use to your family.

PRACTICAL PROBLEMS IN THE AFTERMATH

So much that happens after suicide is literally out of your hands. Suicide survivors report a wide range of common problems that seem to plague them during "postvention." I have listed a few of these here, either to forewarn you or to serve as a reference for those you've already encountered.

Relationships with the Police. The police are required

to investigate the suicide in your family just as they would any other violent death. They can't accept your word that it was suicide. They must reach that conclusion on the basis of their own investigation. Survivors are often hurt by these official actions, as well you may have been. You may have even been a temporary suspect in the death of your family member. In the course of their duties, the police will often unintentionally increase the psychological injury to the survivors of suicide.

In his book *After Suicide* (John Wiley & Sons, 1973), Samuel Wallace points out several instances where much insensitivity occurred on the part of the police. He tells of situations where the police illegally collected "evidence" from the home of the deceased. Other questionable actions included calling a mortician without consulting the family and preventing the family members from seeing the body. In one case, the police retained the body of a drowning victim for a month, until it could be positively identified. Many survivors feel that the "official" presence of the police violates their privacy. Children can also be frightened by the presence of a house full of uniformed officers.

I am glad to say that all the survivors whom I interviewed reported excellent relations with the police. In Louisville, the police department employs full-time chaplains to assist in cases like these. This is commendable, especially in situations where a family has no minister or where pastors refuse to get involved. If the police were helpful to you, why not let them know how much you appreciate their kindness? If you have suggestions as to how they might improve their relations with other survivors, be sure to share those. The police need to hear your perspective. And they'll probably listen to you, because you've been there.

Dealing with the Funeral Director. In his study of the widows of suicides, Wallace found that, with one exception, *all* the spouses felt exploited by the morticians involved in the aftermath. These funeral directors charged widows for placing obituaries in the paper, something the women themselves could have done for free. The morticians made their own investigations into what life insurance was in force, and then charged accordingly. In some cases, they were even able to collect their money directly from the Social Security or Veterans Administrations. In my interviews, I heard gruesome stories about inexperienced and uneducated hired hands who did a haphazard job of cleaning up the remains from a suicide, which resulted in great mental anguish for the family.

These negative reports do not describe all funeral directors everywhere, to be sure. Many trained professionals serve in this capacity, and they do excellent work in assisting families during this difficult time. These cases do point up, however, that morticians are as uncomfortable with suicide as most other people are. And their hired hands may be totally untrained in dealing with such sensitive issues. I cite these situations to remind you that you were and are in charge of all these arrangements. It's your money: don't let anyone manhandle you or your assets in the name of providing a service.

Inquests and Autopsies. Coroners' inquests and autopsies are standard procedures following suicide. Yet both are possible breeding grounds for ill will among surviving families.

Survivors interviewed in one study five years after the death were still upset about the "judicial" atmosphere of the inquest. They felt that they had all been on trial, and this remained a touchy area for them long afterward.

What causes such negative reactions to these legally required procedures? For one thing, inquests often cause delays in funeral arrangements. This stretches out the period of shock and retards necessary grief work. Secondly, inquests are public hearings. Families often feel that their privacy is being invaded: outsiders are able to hear all the details of their family turmoil. Thirdly, many people have strong emotional and religious reservations about autopsies being performed. When this decision is not yours to make, it becomes doubly painful.

Life Insurance Problems. Most life insurance policies have suicide clauses that prohibit any claims for suicide during the first two years of the policy life. Even if your policy was in force, and payment is supposed to be forthcoming, you may have difficulty in collecting. Don't try to hassle the company alone: get a lawyer at the first sign of delays, or call Legal Aid if you can't afford legal counsel. You should not have any problems collecting benefits from the Social Security Administration, since they do not discriminate against the families of suicides.

Newspaper Accounts. The print media too often operate with a double standard in their obituary policies. For instance, the Louisville *Courier-Journal* does not routinely list the cause of death in its death notices. Yet it always indicates when a death has resulted from suicide. Newspaper announcements seem to be a source of anguish for many survivors. Most object to them, for several reasons. They are often inaccurate and sensational, especially if the deceased was a public figure. If a family is trying to "keep an impossible secret," then the death notice lets the word out. The family sees this as an unwelcome intrusion into a private tragedy.

I suggest that you contact your paper about its handling of the suicide of your family member. Your remarks, whether pro or con, may well be the catalyst for a change in policy toward greater consistency in the reporting of deaths.

Monument Sellers. If you haven't yet contacted or been approached by those who sell grave markers, then be prepared. You will hear from them. Ask plenty of questions, and set your own limits. You aren't required to purchase a monument, no matter what the pitch may be. If you don't want to sink a massive sum of money in a gravestone, don't buy one. And don't let anyone appeal to your guilt in order to sell you something.

Your Will. If you didn't have a will before the death of your spouse, you need one now. If you are also a single parent now, you will especially want to see your lawyer about drawing up a will that will adequately distribute your estate, including any insurance claims from the suicide. This is one of the most tangible ways for you to express your love and support for your fellow survivors.

Rejoining the Fragments

You've made it to the end of this little exercise in "postvention." Despite all the obstacles, in spite of all those who didn't think you could be, you are a survivor! You have set in motion a growing life-force within yourself that will continue to keep you going in the months ahead. You've come through the valley of the shadow of death.

Now you have a chance to put your life back together again. In the words of the Persian poet Omar Khayyám, you can "grasp this sorry Scheme of Things entire . . . and then re-mould it nearer to the Heart's Desire" (Omar Khayyám, *The Rubáiyát*, tr. by Edward Fitzgerald). Along with all the Humpty Dumptys who have "had a great fall," you may have felt that your life was permanently shattered into fragments that not even the king's horses and men could rejoin. But I have good news for you. You are not at the mercy of the grave. Death's tentative victory over your life can be reversed in the face of invigorating hope. Death's "two-pronged" sting, which causes not only the dying but also the survivors to suffer, need no longer seem fatal for you. You're going to make it through this tragedy because of who you are.

No other promise makes sense to me. No other hope sounds convincing. As Robert Kavanaugh says: "There is no abiding answer, no consistent comfort, unless the survivor takes time to find the bricks for rebuilding within himself" (Robert E. Kavanaugh, *Facing Death*, p. 162; Penguin Books, 1974).

May this book contribute to the mortar of hope that will hold together the structure of your new life. Brave journey and Godspeed in the building!

7. Anniversary Memorial Service

CALL TO WORSHIP *(Pastor):* Jesus said: "I am the resurrection and the life; he who believes in me, though he die, yet shall he live, and whoever lives and believes in me shall never die. . . . And as for the resurrection of the dead, have you not read what was said to you by God, 'I am the God of Abraham, and the God of Isaac, and the God of Jacob?' He is not God of the dead, but of the living." *(John* 11:25–26; *Matt.* 22:31–32)

PRAYER *(Pastor):* God of mercy and compassion: you have watched over this family in the past year. Out of terrible tragedy you have brought goodness and grace to their lives. You have surrounded them with a sense of your present love, and held them in faith. Though they were lost in grief, they found you and were comforted. They have come today to close their wounds and bind up their broken hearts. Guide them and all of us as we worship you today, through Christ Jesus our Lord, who was dead, but lives and rules this world with you. Amen.

HYMN: "O God, Our Help in Ages Past" (Isaac Watts—William Croft) *or:* "There Is a Balm in Gilead" (Traditional Spiritual)

or: "God Will Take Care of You" (Civilla Martin—Stillman Martin)

LITANY OF THANKSGIVING *(Family)*

Leader (Selected family member): Give thanks to the Lord, for he has been good to us.

Family: His love is everlasting.

Leader: Come, let us praise our God of mercy and compassion.

Family: Let us come to him with thanksgiving.

Leader: For helping us survive the tragedy of suicide,

Family: We thank you, Lord.

Leader: For forgiving, loving, and watching over our loved one, _____ *(Name),*

Family: We thank you, Lord.

Leader: For our friends who helped us through the aftermath,

Family: We thank you, Lord.

Leader: For the love and concern that we share as a family, and for our unity,

Family: We thank you, Lord.

Leader: Above all, O God, we thank you for your Son Jesus Christ, who lived and died and lives again for our salvation; for our hope in him, for the joy of serving him, for the promise of a future with you.

Family: We thank and praise you, God our Father, for all your goodness to us in the past year.

Leader: Give thanks to our God, for he has been good to us.

Family: And his love is everlasting.

SHARING OF MEMORIES *(Family members and others)*

COMMITTAL OF THE MEMORY:

Pastor: Thank God, the God and Father of our Lord Jesus Christ, that in his great mercy we have been born again into a life full of hope, through Christ's rising from the dead. "Do not be afraid. I am the first and the last. I am the living one; for I was dead and now I am alive for evermore. Because I live, you shall live also."

Family: Almighty Goa, we commend to you now our grief in the death of _____ (Name), trusting your love and mercy toward our loved one. Remove from us all our remaining guilt, our anger, our depression, and our blame. Cast out our fear with your perfect love. Heal our wounds, O God, and give us hope for the living of these days, through our Lord Jesus Christ. Amen.

Pastor: All thanks to God, who gives us the victory through Jesus Christ our Lord!

CLOSING HYMN: "My Faith Looks Up to Thee" (Ray Palmer —Lowell Mason)

BENEDICTION *(Everyone):* Now to him who is able to keep us from falling and to present us without blemish before the presence of his glory with rejoicing, to the only God, our Savior through Jesus Christ our Lord, be glory, majesty, dominion, and authority, before all time and now and forever. Amen. *(Jude* 24, 25)

(Service adapted from elements of *The Worshipbook,* Westminster Press, 1970.)

For Further Reading

Chapter 1. GETTING THE FACTS STRAIGHT

Alvarez, A. *The Savage God: A Study of Suicide.* Bantam Books, 1972.

Frederick, Calvin J., and Lague, Louise. *Dealing with the Crisis of Suicide.* (Public Affairs Pamphlet No. 406A). Public Affairs Commission, 1972.

Menninger, Karl. *Man Against Himself.* Harcourt, Brace & World, 1938, 1966.

Perlin, Seymour, ed. *A Handbook for the Study of Suicide.* Oxford University Press, 1975.

Shneidman, Edwin S. "The Enemy." *Psychology Today,* Vol. 4 (Aug. 1970), pp. 37–41, 62–66.

————. and Farberow, Norman L. *Some Facts About Suicide: Causes and Prevention.* Bethesda, Md.: National Institute of Mental Health, 1961.

————. "Suicide." In *Taboo Topics,* ed. by Norman L. Farberow. Atherton Press, 1963. Pp. 33–43.

————. "Suicide Statistics: The Hidden Dimensions." *Psychology Today,* Vol. 11 (Jan. 1978), p. 74.

Chapter 2. COPING WITH ACUTE GRIEF: WHAT TO EXPECT

Bernstein, Joanne E. *Loss and How to Cope with It.* Seabury Press, 1977.

Cain, Albert C., ed. *Survivors of Suicide.* Charles C Thomas, 1972.
Caine, Lynn. *Widow.* William Morrow & Co., 1974.
Claypool, John. *Tracks of a Fellow Struggler: How to Handle Grief.* Word Books, 1974.
Freese, Arthur. *Help for Your Grief.* Schocken Books, 1977.
Glick, Ira O. et al. *The First Year of Bereavement.* John Wiley & Sons, 1974.
Hinton, John. *Dying.* 2d ed. Penguin Books, 1972.
Schiff, Harriet Sarnoff. *The Bereaved Parent.* Crown Publishers, 1977.

Chapter 4. HELPING YOUR CHILDREN IN THE AFTERMATH

For You

Grollman, Earl. *Talking About Death: A Dialogue Between Parent and Child.* New ed. Beacon Press, 1976.
———. *Explaining Death to Children.* Beacon Press, 1967.
Jackson, Edgar N. *Telling a Child About Death.* Channel Press, 1965.
Langone, John. *Death Is a Noun.* Little, Brown & Co., 1972.
Mitchell, Marjorie E. *The Child's Attitude Towards Death.* Schocken Books, 1967.
Wechsler, James A. et al. *In a Darkness.* W. W. Norton, & Co., 1972.
White, Dorothy. *From Two to Five.* Oxford University Press, 1954.
Wolf, Anna W. *Helping Your Child to Understand Death.* Child Study Association of America, 1958.

For Your Child

Armstrong, William. *The Mills of God.* Doubleday & Co., 1973. (Ages 11 and up). A lonely boy, affected by the Depression and the fatal illness of his brother, considers suicide when he must give up a beloved dog.
Cleaver, Vera and Bill. *Grover.* J. B. Lippincott Co., 1970 (Ages

10–14). The process of accepting a mother's suicide, chosen instead of death from cancer.

Platt, Kin. *Chloris and the Creeps.* Chilton Book Co., 1973 (Ages 9–13). The suicide of her father continues to cause severe problems for Chloris in this exploration of denial.